S0-BDN-997

H

AVENUE

TROPICANA

PARADISE

G

F

EAST

AVENUE

E

TROPICANA

D

Harrah's/
Imperial Palace

Flamingo/
Caesars Palace

Bally's/
Paris Las Vegas

MGM
Grand

**The Auto
Collections**
1

**Paris
Las Vegas**
18

**Miracle
Mile**
19

**Planet
Hollywood**
19

**Lion
Habitat**
12

VEGAS

LAS

**Caesars Palace
& the Forum**
3

Bellagio
2

CityCenter
5

**New York-
New York**
17

Excalibur
8

Luxor
13

**Shark
Reef**
21

LAS VEGAS BOULEVARD SOUTH

& the Secret Garden

C

9

10

11

2⁵ Fodor's BEST
Las Vegas

by Jackie Staddon and Hilary Weston

Fodor's Travel Publications
New York • Toronto • London • Sydney • Auckland
www.fodors.com

Contents

KEY TO SYMBOLS

- 🗺 Map reference to the accompanying pull-out map
- ✉ Address
- ☎ Telephone number
- ⏰ Opening/closing times
- 🍴 Restaurant or café
- Ⓡ Nearest monorail station
- 🚌 Nearest bus/trolley route
- ⛴ Nearest riverboat or ferry stop

ENTERTAINMENT 124

Whether you're after a cultural fix or just want a place to relax with a drink after a hard day's sightseeing, we've made the best choices for you.

EAT 136

Uncover great dining experiences, from a quick bite at lunch to top-notch evening meals.

SLEEP 150

We've brought together the best hotels in the city, whatever budget you're on.

NEED TO KNOW 160

The practical information you need to make your trip run smoothly.

PULL-OUT MAP

The pull-out map accompanying this book is a comprehensive street plan of the city. We've given grid references within the book for each sight and listing.

- ♿ Facilities for visitors with disabilities
- 🛈 Tourist information
- ❓ Other practical information
- ▷ Further information

- 🖐 Admission charges:
  Very expensive (over \$50),
  Expensive (\$21–\$50),
  Moderate (\$7–\$20) and
  Inexpensive (under \$7)

Introducing Las Vegas

 Las Vegas is the entertainment capital of the world, where sleep is a mere inconvenience interrupting a continuous stream of fun and hedonism, and where everything is bigger, louder, flashier and trashier than anywhere else in the world.

From the moment you cruise into town it will strike you that this is like no other place. The scale of everything is overwhelming, and The Strip (Las Vegas Boulevard South) in all its blazing glory is a thing of wonderment. Where else can you capture a skyscape that includes the Eiffel Tower, St. Mark's Campanile, an Egyptian pyramid and the Statue of Liberty on the same street? Prepare yourself for a fantasy world made real: volcanoes erupt, seductive sirens lure pirates to a watery fate, and Roman statues come alive.

Evolving from the early saloons, the first casinos and hotels were built in the Downtown area in the 1930s, followed by the expansion of The Strip in the 1940s. Since the late 1980s, mega-hotels have emerged, combining with casinos and theaters to offer the complete experience for gamers and vacationers alike. So what continues to bring millions of visitors here annually—gambling millions of dollars in the process? Las Vegas is an ever-evolving metropolis with a restless spirit that is part of its electric appeal. Hotels are regularly being torn down to make way for brand-new ideas, and entertainment programs constantly change. Vegas now boasts some of the top restaurants in the world, many run by celebrity chefs, and most top fashion designer names have made their mark on the shopping scene.

You might be forgiven for believing Las Vegas is not synonymous with culture and outdoor adventure, but beyond the neon there are some great museums and galleries, and ballet and opera blend perfectly with light entertainment. A few miles away from the man-made wonders are dramatic canyons, dams and sparkling lakes, and the terrain lends itself to some of the finest golf courses. No matter how you spend your time here, this crazy city will never let you forget that the driving force is gambling.

FACTS AND FIGURES

- There are more than 15,000 miles (24,100km) of neon tubing in The Strip and Downtown Las Vegas.
- There are around 315 weddings per day in Vegas.
- There are more than 200,000 slot machines to take your cash.
- On average, each visitor to Las Vegas spends US$482 on gambling.

RAT PACK MEETS VEGAS

In the 1960s, Las Vegas was dominated by a group of singing and acting stars. Frank Sinatra first performed at the Sands Hotel in 1960, with John F. Kennedy in the audience. Thereafter, Sinatra, along with Dean Martin, Sammy Davis Jr., Peter Lawford and Joey Bishop— collectively known as the Rat Pack—dominated the scene and drew the crowds in droves.

TYING THE KNOT IN STYLE

Thousands of people are following in the footsteps of the rich and famous and saying "I do" in Vegas. Famous couples such as Elvis and Priscilla Presley, and Bruce Willis and Demi Moore, have been joined by Mr. and Mrs. Average from countries as far apart as Britain and Japan, to get married in some of the 50 or so wedding chapels (▷ 60–61).

HOW IT BEGAN

Spawned from a trading post along the old Spanish Trail, Las Vegas became a popular stop for its freshwater spring. The prospect of gold added to the lure and later the building of the Hoover Dam secured the city's future. The liberal state laws of Nevada allowed the growth of the casinos, and soon the little campsite in the desert developed into a city.

Focus On Playing the Game

Whether you're hoping to hit the jackpot on the high-stakes tables, or just fancy a taste of the "slots," it's worth finding out first what the main games are and picking up a few tips along the way.

The Games

Baccarat Two-card game, largely based on luck, with the aim of getting a hand adding up to a maximum of 9 points, known as a "natural." One player at a time takes on the bank. It is often given a sophisticated image, with dealers dressed in tuxedos, and played at a table away from the rest of the casino. Best places to play are Monte Carlo, MGM Grand, Palace Station, Treasure Island, The Venetian.

Blackjack Card game, one of the many variations of Pontoon, or 21. Played at a special semicircular table, with five to nine players competing against the dealer. Best places to play are Cannery, El Cortez, Four Queens, Imperial Palace, Terrible's.

Craps Fast, exciting and one of the most popular games, with one player at a time rolling two dice at a special table, holding 12–20 players, and controlled by a "boxman," who stands between the two dealers and monitors the play. To win at craps, the ultimate aim is to roll a 7. Best place to play is Casino Royale (opposite The Mirage).

Keno Similar to bingo, it originated in China. It's a very popular, easy and informal game, but with odds heavily stacked in favor of the house. Best places to play are Flamingo, Orleans, Palace Station, Silverton.

Pai Gow Two-handed poker, based on an original Chinese domino game, with six players taking on the banker. Best places to play are Bellagio, Fitzgeralds.

Roulette Possibly the most famous casino game, betting on a little ball landing in a numbered slot in a spinning wheel. It is played with special chips, with each player having a

Las Vegas is not called the entertainment capital of the world for nothing. Nevada law permits a wide variety of gaming, including traditional card and dice table

different color. If you win and want to cash in your winnings, the dealer will exchange these for winning chips, which you take to a casino cashier. Best places to play are Mirage, Terrible's, Wild Wild West (at Days Inn LV).

Slots These are highly sophisticated computerized machines, paying jackpots of up to $10,000 or more. Serious players guard their machines jealously—if you're playing for hours and need a food or toilet break, ask an attendant to look after your slot for you (a tip is expected). Best places to play are Silverton, Slots a Fun (2890 Las Vegas Boulevard, opposite Circus Circus), Tuscany.

Texas Hold 'Em Five-card game played against the dealer, and currently the most popular form of poker, thanks to free online games, with a wide range of betting limits, from $1 or $2 up to $25,000. Best places to play are The Venetian, Bellagio.

Video Poker Extremely popular and fast version of the classic card game. It is played at a machine and is great if you don't want to sit down with experienced poker players. Best places to play are Palms, South Point.

Lessons
Lessons are available around the clock, based on availability. Dealers often give advice during live games. The Venetian also offers individual and group lessons for Texas Hold 'Em.

Do's and Don'ts
● Choose which game to play and learn the rules first.
● Set a limit to how much you're going to spend before you start playing, and stick to it.
● Check if drinks offered by the waitresses as you play are free—they often are.
● Keep your money safe, within your sight and reach at all times.
● By law, players have to be 21 or older to gamble in Las Vegas casinos.

games, slot machines of virtually every type, race and sports books, high-tech electronic gambling devices and international games of chance

Top Tips For...

These great suggestions will help you tailor your ideal visit to Las Vegas, no matter how you choose to spend your time.

...Something for Free
You can't help but be drawn to the spectacular **Bellagio Fountains** (▷ 16–17).
Take a trip downtown to see the **Fremont Street Experience** (▷ 30–31), a dazzling display of images cast on an LED-light roof.
Visit one of the free live animal attractions, such as the **Lion Habitat** (▷ 36–37) at the MGM Grand.

...Getting the Heart Pumping
Great for an adrenalin rush, brave the thrill rides at the **Stratosphere Tower** (▷ 56–57).
The **Roller Coaster** at New York-New York (▷ 47) is an exhilarating experience.
Take to the sky in a helicopter or small plane for a bird's-eye view of the **Hoover Dam** (▷ 32).

...Hitting the Shopping Malls
At **Fashion Show Mall** (▷ 67) you'll find the leading US department stores and lots more.
For a true smorgasbord of shopping deals, head for one of the outlet malls, such as **Las Vegas Premium Outlets** (▷ 120).
Entertainment and retail therapy go hand-in-hand at **Miracle Mile** (▷ 50–51).
Sample unique shopping under an artificial sky at **The Forum Shops** (▷ 18–19).
You will almost believe you are in Venice at the **Grand Canal Shoppes** (▷ 119).

...Being Pampered
Travel from the airport to your hotel in a **stretch limousine** or **Hummer** (▷ 167).
Check in at one of the most luxurious resorts, like the **Bellagio** (▷ 16–17).
Indulge yourself in ultimate pampering at **Nurture, the Spa at Luxor** (▷ 72).

Clockwise from top: The Bellagio's spectacular "dancing fountains" should not be missed; Caesars Palace at night; a roulette table in Paris Las Vegas; models on the

...Delectable Hot Spots

Dine in restaurants created by celebrity chefs—try **Bradley Ogden** (▷ 141) at Caesars Palace, **Michael Mina** (▷ 146) at Bellagio and Thomas Keller's **Bouchon** (▷ 141) at The Venetian.

Take advantage of some of the city's finest French cuisine; **Joël Robuchon** at the MGM Grand (▷ 144–145) is one of the best. Enjoy the Bellagio's fountain show from **Mon Ami Gabi** (▷ 146) at Paris Las Vegas. For a sweet finish to your culinary tour, have dessert at the **Jean-Philippe Patisserie** at ARIA, in the CityCenter (▷ 144).

...High-Energy Dance Clubs

Show your moves on one of the four dance floors at **Studio 54** (▷ 134).

For top chart hits and great views over The Strip, try **Pure** (▷ 134).

For new innovations that will impress, join the sophisticated crowd at **Tryst** (▷ 135).

...World-Class Entertainment

See a Broadway production: **Phantom of the Opera** is still going strong at The Venetian (▷ 134).

Reserve well in advance for a close encounter with a megastar; check out the **Colosseum** (▷ 129) to see who's making headlines. Be amazed by one of the many **Cirque du Soleil** (▷ 132) productions in town.

...Some Casino Action

Join the high rollers at **The Venetian** (▷ 58–59), watched over by Tiepolos and Titians.

Cocktail waitresses in togas will serve you drinks at **Caesars Palace** (▷ 18–19) while you place your bets.

Tuxedo-backed chairs set the tone at **New York-New York** (▷ 46–47), against the backdrop of the Big Apple.

catwalk at the Fashion Show Mall, the first mall on The Strip; a stretch limousine is one of the best ways to get around town; the Lion Habitat at the MGM Grand

Timeline

1829 The spring at Las Vegas is discovered by a Mexican scout, Rafael Rivera, riding with a 60-strong trading party that had strayed from the Spanish Trail en route to Los Angeles.

1855 Mormon settlers build a fort at Las Vegas. They stay for three years, until Native American raids drive them out.

EARLY BEGINNINGS

In prehistoric times the land on which the city stands was a marshy area that supported vigorous plant life, but the water eventually receded and the arid landscape we see today was created. However, underground water occasionally surfaced to nourish an oasis on the site where Vegas now stands, known at that time only to the area's Native Americans. Archaeological finds just 10 miles (16km) northwest of Vegas have identified one of the oldest sites of human habitation in the United States. Items have been found at Tule Springs that date from around 11,000 to 14,000 years ago.

1905 On May 15, the railroad arrives, and trackside lots in what is now the Fremont Street area sell like hot cakes.

1910 Gambling is made illegal in the state of Nevada, sending the games underground.

1931 The Nevada legislature passes a bill to allow gambling, and El Rancho becomes the first casino to open in Las Vegas. Nevada remains the only state to allow casino gambling until 1976, when casinos are introduced to Atlantic City.

1940s A building boom expands Las Vegas and more casinos come to town, along with organized crime. Vegas is ruled by the Mafia for decades.

1946 The Flamingo, one of the foremost early casinos, opens its doors. It's financed by Benjamin "Bugsy" Siegel of the Meyer Lansky gang.

"Bugsy" Siegel's Flamingo Hotel, c.1947

Demolition of the Stardust Resort and Casino on The Strip in 2007

1959 The Tropicana Hotel buys the American rights to the Parisian Folies Bergere show—it runs until 2009, with some 40,000 spectators a month.

1960s The Rat Pack (Frank Sinatra, Dean Martin, Sammy Davis Jr. et al.) arrive, setting the pattern for superstar entertainment.

1967 The Nevada legislature approves a bill that allows publicly traded corporations to obtain gambling licenses. Legitimate money begins to loosen the Mafia's hold.

1976 Casino gambling is legalized in Atlantic City; Las Vegas has competition.

1990s Las Vegas begins to promote family attractions. Ever bigger, more fantastic architecture starts to dominate The Strip.

2001 Wayne Newton, "Mr Las Vegas," signs a lucrative contract with the Stardust Hotel.

2004 A new state-of-the art monorail opens.

2005 On May 15, Las Vegas celebrates its 100th birthday.

2007 Opened in 1958, the legendary Stardust hotel is the latest hotel to be demolished.

2009 The world economic downturn bites in Las Vegas. Casino projects are frozen, tourist numbers are down and there is an unemployment crisis.

2012 Opening of the $485 million Smith Center for the Performing Arts, which will host major Broadway shows, as well as orchestral, operatic and dance performances.

EVERYONE'S A WINNER

The fortunes of Las Vegas owe a lot to entrepreneur and property developer Steve Wynn (b.1942). Raised in a Jewish family in New York, he took over the family bingo business in the 1960s and moved to Las Vegas in 1967. His first major venture here was to revamp the Golden Nugget. His next project was The Mirage casino resort, which opened in 1989, followed by Treasure Island in 1993. Next came Bellagio, spawning a new breed of luxury resorts. When his company Mirage Resorts was sold to MGM in 2000, he turned his energies to his most expensive development, the Wynn Las Vegas, followed by the Encore next door. Wynn became a billionaire by 2004 and is an ardent art collector.

Steve Wynn, CEO of Wynn Resorts

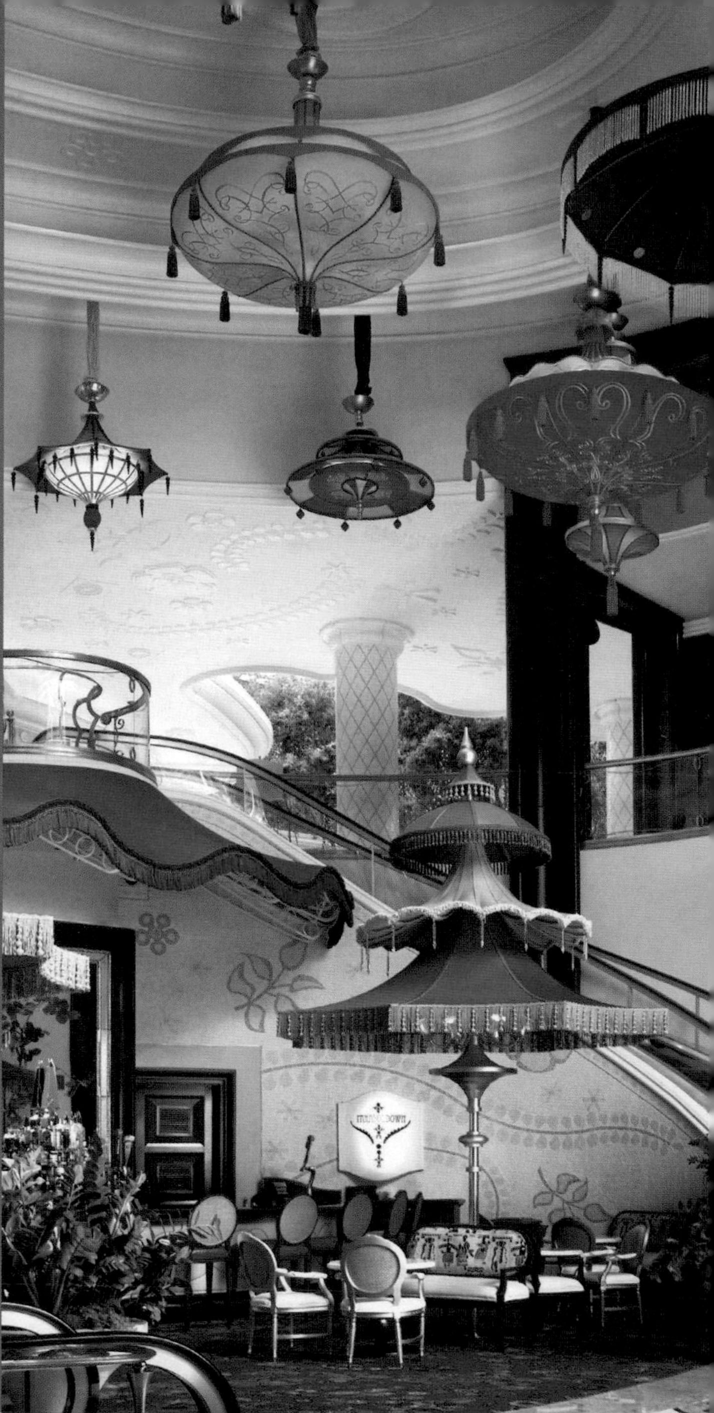

Top 25

This section contains the must-see Top 25 sights and experiences in Las Vegas. They are listed alphabetically, and numbered so you can locate them on the inside front cover map.

TOP 25

DID YOU KNOW?

● Because of his germ phobia, Howard Hughes installed an air-purification system into his 1954 Chrysler that cost more than the car.

● President Truman's 1950 Lincoln Cosmopolitan had a gold-plated interior.

● The 1933 Silver Arrow displayed at the museum is one of only three still in existence today.

The fifth level of the Imperial Palace parking facility takes on a rather different look from the other floors—this luxurious space displays a stunning collection of classic and special-interest cars, spanning a century of motoring.

Plush parking You could easily spend hours here, in what is one of the finest and largest automobile showrooms in the world. When it opened in 1981 the collection had 200 vehicles; since then, this number has increased to an impressive 700, although only around 250 are displayed at one time. There are gleaming examples of all those classics that generations of drivers have yearned for, there are rare and exclusive models, and there are cars that represent landmarks in vehicle

Clockwise from far left: Volkswagen Micro Bus Camper and Beetle; 1959 Rolls-Royce Silver Cloud I Drophead Coupe; 1951 Talbot-Lago T 26 Grand Sport Saoutchik Coupe; 1933 Pierce-Arrow Silver Arrow; Rolls-Royce Silver Cloud I Sedanca Coupe; 1956 Lincoln Premiere Convertible

construction and technology. A significant acquisition for the exhibition here is the world's largest collection of Model J. Duesenbergs.

Famous and infamous owners Some of the vehicles that hold the greatest fascination are those that are noteworthy because of the people who drove them. You might see Marilyn Monroe's pink 1955 Lincoln Capri convertible, an armor-plated 1939 Mercedes-Benz used by Adolph Hitler, and cars owned by Al Capone, Elvis Presley, Benito Mussolini and James Cagney. There's no certainty about what will be on show because this is not exactly a straightforward museum, and the collection is not necessarily a permanent one. All of the exhibits are for sale, and serious buyers may well be among your fellow browsers on the lot.

THE BASICS

www.autocollections.com

➕ D8–D9

✉ Imperial Palace, 3535 Las Vegas Boulevard South

☎ 702/794-3174

🕐 Daily 10–6

🍽 Several cafés and restaurants at the Imperial Palace

🚌 Harrah's/Imperial Palace

🚗 Deuce

💲 Inexpensive

❓ Gift shop

HIGHLIGHTS

- Fountain show
- Gallery of Fine Art
- Botanical garden
- The lobby

The Italianate image for this $1.6 billion hotel, deemed to be one of the most opulent resorts in the world, was inspired by the village of Bellagio, on the shores of Italy's Lake Como.

A touch of class A 10-acre (4ha) man-made lake at the front of the hotel sets the stage for the elegance, art and grandeur that awaits you inside. The dazzling front lobby has an 18ft (5.5m) ceiling with a chandelier of glass flowers called Fiori di Como suspended in the middle, designed by glass sculptor Dale Chihuly. All this splendor is enhanced by the wonderful botanical garden, set under a glass atrium.

Fountains at Bellagio During the computer-controlled, choreographed fountain show,

Clockwise from far left: View of the Bellagio from the Eiffel Tower at Paris Las Vegas; the Bellagio's pools; Dale Chihuly's spectacular chandelier of glass flowers; the entrance to the Gallery of Fine Art; the plants in the botanical garden and conservatory are changed seasonally

millions of gallons of water are sprayed to heights of 240ft (73m) above the hotel's massive lake. The system uses individually programmed water jets and atomizing nozzles that create an atmospheric fog on the lake; some jets can change the direction of the water, giving a dancing effect. The show is enhanced by the integrated illumination that starts after dark, and by the audio system, with music ranging from Pavarotti to Sinatra.

So much The casino oozes sophistication, its slot machines encased in marble and wood. Bellagio is proud of its Gallery of Fine Art (▷ 66–67), and its theater was styled after the Paris Opera for Cirque du Soleil's "O" (▷ 132). The glass-enclosed Via Bellagio shopping mall (▷ 123) has exclusive boutiques.

THE BASICS

www.bellagio.com

✚ C9–D9

✉ 3600 Las Vegas Boulevard South

☎ 702/693-7111

🕐 Fountains: Mon–Fri 3pm–midnight, Sat–Sun 12–12; every half-hour to 8pm then every 15 min (may be canceled in high winds)

🍴 Several cafés and restaurants

🚌 Bally's/Paris

🚍 Deuce

♿ Fountains: free

❓ No under-18s are allowed in Bellagio unless accompanied by a registered guest

HIGHLIGHTS

● The Forum Shops mall
● Festival of Fountains and Atlantis show
● A performance at the Colosseum

So you're in Las Vegas, and the thing you most want to do is spend a day shopping for Italian-designer chic surrounded by the historic buildings of ancient Rome? No problem. It's all here at Caesars Palace.

Classical architecture You could easily believe that you have been transported to the Italian capital, amid architecture that spans the period from 300BC to AD1700. The grounds are filled with reproductions of Roman statues, marble columns and colonnades, and toga-clad cocktail waitresses and costumed centurions tend to your every need in the exciting casino.

The Forum Visit the phenomenal retail concourse, The Forum Shops. Wander in and out of such stores as Versace and Roberto

Clockwise from far left: The Fountain of the Gods; a replica of Michelangelo's David; nighttime view of the hotel; The Forum Shops mall; a statue of Greek goddesses greets visitors in the lobby of the hotel

Cavalli, or eat at one of the many restaurants. An artificial sky overhead gives the illusion that 24 hours have passed in just one hour. Every hour the Festival of Fountains springs into action, when statues come to life, special effects kick in, and you are entertained by characters from Roman mythology, such as Bacchus and Apollo. In the Roman Great Hall, more special effects and animatronics combine to portray the struggle to rule Atlantis, with the backdrop of a massive marine aquarium.

Star-studded performances The 4,100-seat Colosseum (▷ 129) has hosted big-name shows, including Cher and Elton John. Other attractions include a 3-D IMAX motion simulator where three-dimensional images and sound systems offer a unique experience.

THE BASICS

www.caesarspalace.com

➕ C8–D8

✉ 3570 Las Vegas Boulevard South

☎ 702/731-7110. The Forum: 702/893-4800

🎭 Festival of Fountains/ Atlantis show: daily every hour 10am–11pm

🍴 Several cafés and restaurants

🚌 Flamingo/Caesars

🚍 Deuce

🎟 Festival of Fountains/ Atlantis show: free

- The Canyon Blaster ride
- The Rim Runner ride
- The Chaos ride
- FX Theater
- Big Top circus acts
- The Disk'o ride

- Height restrictions may apply on some rides.
- If you're intending to stay a while at the Adventuredome, the daily pass can save you money.

The circus has come to town. In fact, it arrived here on The Strip in 1968, when Circus Circus opened its doors to provide the city with its first gaming concern offering family entertainment.

Roll up, roll up At first there were no hotel rooms, only a casino and the world's biggest permanent circus tent. Today there are around 1,500 guest rooms behind the first-floor casino, while the upper floor has carnival attractions and arcade games surrounding a circus arena. Acrobats, trapeze artists, aerialists and clowns are just some of the acts that perform daily.

Undercover thrills In 1993 the Adventuredome was added, said to be the biggest indoor theme park in the country,

Clockwise from far left: The breathtaking Rim Runner; Chaos, a truly unpredictable ride; the Canyon Blaster roller coaster is not for the faint-hearted; the iconic clown neon sign; you can't mistake the theme of this hotel; Thunderbirds are go!

covering about 5 acres (2ha) beneath an enormous glass dome. The main thrill rides (for the very brave) include the Canyon Blaster, a massive double-loop, double-corkscrew roller coaster that achieves a top speed of 55mph (88kph); Chaos, which hurls its passengers in all directions as it speeds on its unpredictable course; the Inverter, which literally turns your world upside down; and the Rim Runner, a water ride that includes a breathtaking plunge. For the Disk'o ride you will need a strong stomach, and for the 4-D experience check out the special FX Theater.

Gentler fun There are also less stressful activities. These include team laser tag and a climbing wall, while younger children will love the carousels, bumper cars and miniature golf.

THE BASICS

www.circuscircus.com
➕ E6
✉ 2880 Las Vegas Boulevard South
☎ 702/734-0410. Adventuredome: 702/794-3939
🕐 Midway Circus Acts: every half-hour 11am–midnight. Adventuredome: Mon–Thu 10–6, Fri–Sat 10am–midnight, Sun 10–9 (hours may vary seasonally)
🍴 Several cafés and restaurants
🚌 Sahara
🚍 Deuce
💰 Adventuredome: free admission, charge for rides; daily pass expensive

HIGHLIGHTS

- Viva ELVIS, Cirque du Soleil show
- Crystals mall
- Fine art collection
- Gourmet restaurants

TIP

- Take the free tram to CityCenter which runs from the Bellagio to the Monte Carlo (daily, approx. every 10 minutes, 8am–4am; journey time 2.5 minutes).

This ultra-modern complex of gleaming angular towers is a self-contained city in the heart of The Strip. It's architecturally stunning, setting new standards for style and sophistication.

Layout CityCenter comprises three hotels: the ARIA, Vdara Hotel & Spa and the Mandarin Oriental. The site includes Crystals, the first retail center to be designed by architect Daniel Liebeskind, as well as its own power plant, fire station and tram line. The complex was built with special attention to energy conservation. It uses its excess electricity to provide its hot water, and its stretch limos run on compressed natural gas—a world first. The ARIA, the only casino, is home to the Cirque du Soleil's Viva ELVIS show (▷ 74, 153).

Clockwise from far left: CityCenter at night; Typewriter Eraser by Claes Oldenburg and Coosje van Bruggen; the Las Vegas monorail runs through CityCenter; shopping at the Vdara hotel; reflections of Las Vegas

Arty refuge CityCenter's towers are grouped around spacious plazas and atriums, which are decorated with artworks by internationally acclaimed artists, such as Henry Moore, Claes Oldenburg, Maya Lin, Richard Long, Nancy Rubins and Frank Stella. Giant aerial sculptures hang from cavernous hallways, and miniature whirlpools gyrate inside glass tubes embedded in the sidewalk. Among the most spectacular pieces are Nancy Rubins' *Big Edge*—a spiky sculpture of boats and canoes outside the Vdara; Maya Lin's *Silver River*, suspended over the ARIA's registration desk; and a large marble sculpture by Henry Moore in The Park, between the ARIA and Crystals. The wide open public spaces offer a more relaxed experience, with modern art on display and fountains that both stimulate and soothe the senses.

THE BASICS

www.citycenter.com

✚ C9–C10

✉ 3720 Las Vegas Boulevard South

🍴 Numerous restaurants and cafés

🚇 Bally's/Paris

🚌 Deuce

6 Dolphin Habitat and the Secret Garden

● Watching the dolphins frolic
● If you're lucky, being there when a baby dolphin has just been born
● Rays touch pool

TIPS

● You can stay as long as you like, so be patient and you are more likely to observe a special moment.
● If they aren't doing it already, ask the keepers to play ball with the dolphins.

Here you can be entertained by marine mammals playing in their natural environment or get close up with some of the rarest and most exotic animals in the world, all in one afternoon.

Dolphins at play To the rear of The Mirage (▷ 42–43), the Dolphin Habitat's intent is to provide a happy and nurturing environment for Atlantic bottlenose dolphins and increase public awareness and the commitment to protect and conserve marine animals in general. You can watch these amazing mammals frolic across a shimmering lagoon or see them below from the viewing gallery, and learn more about marine mammals on a 15-minute tour. The dolphins breed regularly, so you might be fortunate enough to see a baby at play. All the

Clockwise from far left: An Atlantic bottlenose dolphin at Dolphin Habitat; feline residents in Siegfried and Roy's Secret Garden include rare white tigers and lions

dolphins have names and respond to their keeper's instructions.

Secret Garden Next to the Dolphin Habitat, Siegfried and Roy's Secret Garden re-creates a jungle haven for five rare breeds of big cats: white lions of Timbavati, heterozygous Bengal tigers (with both tawny and white genes), the royal white tigers of Nevada, a panther and a snow leopard. The newest additions arrived in July 2010: Mohan and Majestic, white-striped tiger cubs. The cubs' parents carry the rare recessive gene that produces the white offspring. It's a breeding program that is part of an ongoing conservation plan to maintain these beautiful animals. When there are cubs in the garden a special nursery area is created for them and they are just adorable to watch.

THE BASICS

www.miragehabitat.com
➕ C8
✉ The Mirage, 3400 Las Vegas Boulevard South
☎ 702/791-7188
🕐 Mon–Fri 11–5.30, Sat–Sun 10–5.30 (longer hours in summer); last admission 30 min before closing
🍴 Several cafés and restaurants at The Mirage
🚇 Harrah's/Imperial Palace
🚌 Deuce
💰 Moderate

HIGHLIGHTS

● Fremont Street
Experience
● Main Street Station
● Golden Nugget casino
(▷ 68)
● The Arts Factory (▷ 66)

TIP

● Some of the carts around
Fremont have unusual gift
items for sale.

With its old-world appeal, Downtown is
where the spirit of Las Vegas's humble
beginnings still lives on through original
casino hotels like the Plaza, the Golden
Nugget and the Golden Gate, the city's
oldest hotel.

Origins Centered on Fremont Street between
Main and 9th, the streets of Downtown are
narrower, more low-key and less glamorous
than those on The Strip. In the 1920s, Fremont
Street was the first street in Las Vegas to be
paved and have traffic lights, and by the
1930s it had the first licensed gaming hall.
Downtown already had 36 years of history as
the commercial heart of Vegas by the time the
first casino resort, El Rancho, was built on The
Strip in 1941.

Clockwise from far left: Vegas Vicki sits atop the Glitter Gulch sign; the Fremont Street Experience; Sam Boyd's casino; Main Street Station boasts Victorian decor, antiques and artifacts; blackjack tables in Main Street Station casino

Revitalization Downtown had lost much of its business to The Strip by the 1990s, but since then the $70 million Fremont Street Experience (▷ 30–31) has succeeded in bringing in the punters once again and putting Glitter Gulch—as it is known—firmly back on the map.

More attractions With its striking Victorian decor and genuine antiques, Main Street Station (▷ 157) has one of the city's best casinos in terms of comfort and atmosphere. Just outside Main Street Station two old rail cars are displayed. One is the *Blackhawk* used by Buffalo Bill Cody to travel with his Wild West Show between 1906 and 1917 and still in its original state. The other, the *Cascade*, is a wonderfully preserved Pullman car built in 1897, complete with original fittings.

THE BASICS

🟦 G2
✉ Centered around Fremont and Main streets
🍴 Numerous
🚌 108, Deuce

HIGHLIGHTS

● Tournament of Kings
● Court Jester's Stage
● 4-D simulator rides

TIPS

● You must be at least 42in (1.06m) tall to go on the motion simulator rides.
● You will need to book well in advance for the Tournament of Kings dinner show.

All the romance and excitement of legendary medieval Europe is re-created at this sparkling castle-shaped hotel, with exciting special effects, sword fights, jousting and jugglers.

Camelot Cross the drawbridge and you enter a world where technology meets the legend of King Arthur. Inside the stone walls, stained glass and heraldic shields set the scene, and strolling costumed performers enhance the atmosphere.

Medieval Village An escalator transports you to the second floor, where you are greeted by a fire-breathing dragon. The main stage presents free shows, including juggling, puppetry and storytelling. On the lower level at the Fun Dungeon there are traditional carnival

Clockwise from left: King Arthur would feel right at home in the Excalibur; inside the hotel lobby; there's something for everyone at the Excalibur; slot machines in the casino; the popular Tournament of Kings show

attractions, state-of-the-art video games and 4-D simulator rides. Castle Walk shops sell medieval-style merchandise, and there are several theme restaurants.

Tournament of Kings This enthralling dinner show revolves around highly skilled stunts—often on horseback—high-tech special effects, wonderful costumes and a stirring musical score. King Arthur and his knights play host to other monarchs across Europe. There's a procession, followed by traditional medieval games of skill, agility, might and endurance. But when the evil Mordred attacks, amid burning fires and accompanied by a dragon, the clash of swords begins. The victor is presented with Excalibur by Merlin and the show ends with more festivities.

THE BASICS

www.excalibur.com

🖽 D10

✉ 3850 Las Vegas Boulevard South

☎ 702/597-7777. Tournament of Kings: 702/597-7600

🕐 Tournament of Kings: Mon, Wed 6pm, Thu–Sun 6 and 8.30pm

🍴 Several cafés and restaurants

🚇 MGM Grand

🚌 Deuce

💷 Tournament of Kings: very expensive, 4-D simulator rides: inexpensive

Head north to the Downtown area after dark to see the only show of its kind in the world—a fantastic light-and-sound show on a massive frame that overarches a five-block area.

High-tech marvel The specifications for the initial display comprised 2 million light bulbs, with strobe lighting added to enhance the disco nights. In 2004, a $17 million upgrade provided a 12.5 million LED light display and a better quality system (to 550,000 watts) for state-of-the-art sound. The Experience is a high-tech phenomenon with the latest computers intertwining the light, visual and audio systems.

Under cover of lightness This glittering spectacular is based on a huge, solid frame

Clockwise from far left: The Fremont Street Experience; Binion's has been in business since 1951; the FSE's light-and-sound show is second to none; Neonopolis Mall, with its historic neons; another spectacular light show

that curves 90ft (27m) above traffic-free Fremont Street, between Main and 4th streets. A number of the Downtown casinos are within this area (▷ 26–27), adding to the overall effect with their illuminated facades. There are 16 massive columns and 43,000 struts supporting the frame, but once the show starts you are totally focused on this breathtaking experience that has been wowing the crowds here since 1995.

By day You might suppose that it's rather dull here during the day, but the display frame shelters a lively shopping mall, the sound system continues to pipe in music to shop by, and there are often free concerts and street performers. A new zip line, 80ft (18m) above the street, offers high-adrenaline thrills.

THE BASICS

www.vegasexperience.com

➕ G3

✉ Fremont Street

☎ 702/678-5600

🕐 Shows nightly at 8.30, 9, 10, 11 and midnight

🍴 Numerous cafés and restaurants

🚌 108, Deuce

♿ Free

10 Hoover Dam and Lake Mead

TOP 25

HIGHLIGHTS

- Guided tour into the Hoover Dam
- Cruising Lake Mead on an organized sightseeing tour

TIPS

- There is a large choice of tours available from Las Vegas (▷ 167).
- The best sightseeing cruise on Lake Mead is the one aboard the *Desert Princess*.
- Tours of the dam leave from the exhibit center at the top of the dam.

It's hard to visit Vegas without feeling some wonderment about the power it must take to light up the town. You'll find some answers at Hoover Dam, and while you're out of the city, enjoy a cruise on the lovely lake it created.

A marvel of engineering Without the Hoover Dam, Las Vegas, as we know it, would not exist. Constructed in the mid-1930s to control flooding on the Colorado River, it also provides drinking water for 25 million people and electricity for half a million homes. It was completed two years ahead of schedule. At the peak of construction over 5,000 people were employed and 96 workers died on the project. Fascinating tours take visitors deep inside the structure to learn about its inner workings.

Clockwise from far left: On the shores of Lake Mead; the Desert Princess tour boat; kayaking on Lake Mead; boats moored at Lake Mead; Hoover Dam, one of the seven engineering wonders of the world; the dam's structural volume surpasses that of the largest pyramid in Egypt

Lovely Lake Mead The damming of the Colorado River between 1935 and 1938 created the second-largest artificial lake in the US, with a vast 550-mile (885km) shoreline. There's a scenic drive along the western side, and the Alan Bible Visitor Center, just west of the dam, has information about waterborne activities. There are five marinas, and you can rent a boat or jet ski, go fishing, water-skiing or swimming. On dry land there are lakeshore walks and facilities for camping and picnicking. Boulder City, on the lake shore, was built to house dam construction workers and was "dry" (no alcohol or gambling). It is the only community in Nevada that still restricts gambling. A new bridge bypassing the dam was built in 2010, helping to ease traffic to and from the Grand Canyon.

THE BASICS

www.usbr.gov/lc/hoover dam; www.nps.gov/lame

🚹 Off map at J3

✉ 30 miles (48km) southeast of Las Vegas

☎ Hoover Dam tours: 702/494-2517. Alan Bible Visitor Center: 702/293-8990. Lake Mead Cruises: 702/293-6180

🕐 Hoover Dam Visitor Center: daily 9–5; Alan Bible Visitor Center: daily 9–4.15

✋ Hoover Dam Visitor Center Tours: expensive. Lake Mead Recreation Area: inexpensive. Lake Mead cruise: expensive

Las Vegas Natural History Museum

HIGHLIGHTS

- Hands-on activity room
- Whales exhibition
- Marine Life Gallery
- Robotic T-Rex and Dinosaur Gallery
- African Galleries

This terrific museum provides a welcome contrast to the high life and glitz of the shows and casinos. There are lots of interactive displays, wildlife exhibits, live animals to pet, animatronic dinosaurs and much more.

Unique items When you consider all the museums in the United States, you might not expect a Las Vegas institution to have something the others don't. However, among the displays here are two particularly rare species—the African water chevrotain (a cross between a pig and a deer) and the Liberian zebra duiker. In addition, there are more than 26 species of stuffed animals mounted in cases, including the largest jaguar ever displayed.

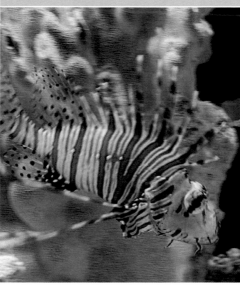

Animated exhibits, live animals and robotic dinosaurs (including a triceratops and a T-Rex), plus a variety of fish and sharks, mounted animals and fossils, make the perfect break from the fantasy world of The Strip

Marine world Opened in 2004, the whales exhibit is part of the Marine Life Gallery and complements the shark displays, which feature live leopard sharks and a shark egg hatchery. There is a scale model of an orca, also known as the killer whale, a melonhead whale and a beluga whale, complete with baby. You can learn about the behavior and conservation of these creatures. Don't miss the re-creation of the jaws of a 50ft-long (15m) prehistoric shark.

Fun with the animals Many of the displays are animated, including five robotic dinosaurs—the 35ft (10.5m) T-Rex is very popular. There are also live animals that visitors are sometimes allowed to pet. The concept is to combine education with fun, and the interactive area is a great place for children.

THE BASICS

www.lvnhm.org
✚ H2
✉ 900 North Las Vegas Boulevard
☎ 702/384-3466
🕐 Daily 9–4
🚌 113
♿ Moderate

This is a remarkable place, where you can get up close to magnificent big cats in the knowledge that their stay in the enclosure will be only slightly longer than yours.

A temporary sojourn Anyone who has qualms about wild animals being caged for human entertainment can rest assured that the lions are brought here for just a short time from their spacious home outside the city. They belong to animal trainer Keith Evans, who makes the trip three times a day to ensure that no cat is in the enclosure for longer than six hours.

Surrounded by lions The three-level, glass-walled structure, reaching a height of more than 35ft (10.5m), is similar in concept to the walk-through tunnels you'll find in big aquariums.

At the Lion Habitat you are literally encircled by lions via a see-through glass walkway tunnel, which can take the weight of an adult lion running at 25mph (40kph)

You will see the animals close up, and can study their every move with perfect clarity as they prowl on either side and even stride across the tunnel roof above your head—and all that separates you is a thick layer of the toughest strengthened glass available. The Lion Habitat has been laid out to resemble the natural landscape the cats would know in the wild, including indigenous foliage, rocks, four separate waterfalls and a pond.

Raised in captivity One of the most famous lions of all time was Metro, whose roar announced every MGM Studio production. Three of his descendants—Goldie, Metro and Baby Lion—are among the collection of more than two dozen big cats, all of which have been raised in captivity by Evans and his wife.

THE BASICS

www.mgmgrand.com

☷ D10

✉ MGM Grand, 3799 Las Vegas Boulevard South

☎ 702/891-1111

🕐 Daily 11–7

🍴 Cafés and restaurants at MGM Grand

🚇 MGM Grand

🚌 Deuce

♿ Free

HIGHLIGHTS

- Bodies...The Exhibition
- *Titanic* exhibition
- Replica sphinx
- Laser light

TIP

- Save your aching feet and take the free monorail to Luxor, which runs between Excalibur and Mandalay Bay.

It may be disconcerting that the Luxor's interior has been stripped of its Egyptian theme to make way for a trendy new image, but don't despair, two exciting exhibitions more than compensate.

Egyptian roots Although more modern attractions are on offer inside, the gigantic black-glass pyramid, with its massive 10-floor replica sphinx at the entrance, still dominates—which is no surprise as it is the main hotel building. An intense narrow spotlight shoots out from the top of the pyramid; claimed to be the strongest beam of light in the world, on a clear night it is visible from outer space.

***Titanic* docks at Luxor** *Titanic*: The Artifact Exhibition takes you on an emotional journey

Clockwise from far left: For a different view of the human form, visit Bodies...The Exhibition; an enormous Sphinx guards the extrance to the Luxor; the Digestive System exhibit; outside Titanic and Bodies...The Exhibition; take a break at the T&T Mexican-style restaurant

back in time to experience the ill-fated ship's maiden voyage. On display are hundreds of authentic objects recovered from *Titanic's* final resting place. A reconstructed ship's bow utilizes a moving lifeboat to gain access on board. Walk through room creations, share in the dramatic stories of the passengers and crew and experience the feel of an iceberg, which set the stage for one of history's greatest tragedies.

Come see what's inside Bodies...The Exhibition is a superb opportunity to see the inner workings of our bodies through actual preserved human bodies, plus more than 260 organs and partial body specimens. This daring attraction is a groundbreaking venture for Las Vegas—a fairly serious experience that will leave you with many lasting thoughts.

THE BASICS

www.luxor.com

🔢 C11–D11

✉ 3900 Las Vegas Boulevard South

☎ 702/262-4000

🕐 *Titanic* and Bodies exhibitions: daily 10–10

🍴 Several cafés and restaurants

🚇 MGM Grand

🚌 Deuce

💲 *Titanic* and Bodies exhibitions: expensive

HIGHLIGHTS

● "The King in Concert"
● "Marry Clooney"
● SCREAM–the Chamber of Horrors

It is fitting that Madame Tussaud's first foray into the United States should be in Las Vegas, a magnet for both the biggest showbiz personalities and the most ardent celebrity-spotters.

Making an impression Madame Tussaud's is the world leader when it comes to making realistic likenesses in wax of the rich, the famous and the infamous. The secret is that they take an impression from the real person, rather than simply use an artist's sculpture, so every detail is absolutely spot on. This can be a rather claustrophobic experience; Napoleon was famously freaked out by it. Today, however, most celebrities regard it as at least one of the signs that they have really made it in the business.

The star-studded cast at Madame Tussaud's includes (clockwise from far left): Hugh Heffner, Frank Sinatra, Louis Armstrong, Muhammad Ali, Liberace, Siegfried and Roy and Marilyn Monroe

Las Vegas legends Not surprisingly, pride of place here goes to the superstars who have made their mark in Vegas—Wayne Newton, Elvis Presley, Engelbert Humperdinck, Tom Jones and the Rat Pack, to name just a few. Among more than 100 other masterfully produced figures is an international cast of movie and TV stars, icons from the music world and sport's big achievers.

Interactive experience Some exhibits allow you to interact with the famous models by taking part in a scenario, such as auditioning in front of Simon Cowell for *American Idol*. The highlight for every woman must be the "Marry Clooney" exhibit, where you put on a wedding gown and walk down the aisle with the gorgeous George himself—in your dreams!

THE BASICS

www.madametussauds.com/lasvegas

☐ D8

✉ The Venetian, 3377 Las Vegas Boulevard South

☎ 702/862-7800

◷ Sun–Thu 10–9.30, Fri–Sat 10am–10.30pm (sometimes closes early for special events)

🍴 Several cafés and restaurants at The Venetian

🚌 Harrah's/Imperial Palace

🚃 Deuce

💰 Expensive

HIGHLIGHTS

● Volcanic eruption
● Secret Garden and white tigers
● Dolphin Habitat

TIP

● Note that the volcano eruption will be canceled during bad weather or high winds.

There is nothing so fascinating as the power of nature, and to watch The Mirage's simulated volcano erupt or come face-to-face with the magnificent wildlife is a highlight that will enhance anyone's day.

Tropical delights This Polynesian-style resort is fronted by cascading waterfalls, tropical foliage and an imitation volcano. As you enter the lobby you can't miss the huge coral-reef aquarium stocked with tropical fish. Venture farther in and you will discover a lush rain forest under a large atrium.

Eruptions to order You can wait years for a real volcano to create its spectacle, but here, in front of The Mirage, you can set your watch by it. The newly renovated spectacular two-minute

Clockwise from far left: The volcano is set to erupt outside The Mirage; The Spa at The Mirage; the Revolution Lounge; waterfalls cascading into the lagoon outside the hotel

show starts with a rumbling sound, then a fog swirls around and a column of smoke and fire shoots more than 12ft (3.5m) into the sky. The show includes the latest special effects, with real flames on the water of the lagoon and state-of-the-art lighting techniques and sound systems. Arrive early to get a front-row position.

Other attractions The Mirage is also home to the Dolphin Habitat and Siegfried and Roy's Secret Garden (▷ 24–25). The habitats serve as educational centers for guests and school children in the community. Since opening in 1997, the Secret Garden has endeavored to renew the public's sense of responsibility to preserve nature. The Cirque du Soleil creation LOVE (▷ 66) is presented at The Mirage and celebrates the musical legacy of The Beatles.

THE BASICS

www.themirage.com

➕ C8–D8

✉ 3400 Las Vegas Boulevard South

☎ 702/791-7111

🕐 Volcanic eruption: daily every hour 6pm–11pm

🍴 Several cafés and restaurants

🚉 Harrah's/Imperial Palace

🚌 Deuce

🌋 Volcanic eruption: free

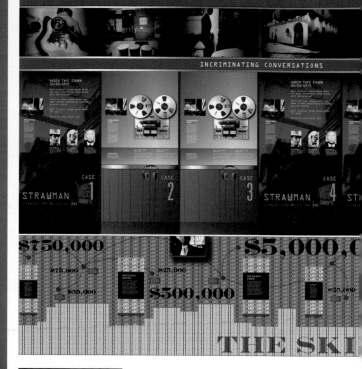

INCRIMINATING CONVERSATIONS

$750,000

THE SKI

HIGHLIGHTS

● The Barber's Chair – where "Murder Inc." mobster Albert Anastasia was shot dead in New York in 1957
● The Colt revolver recovered from the 1929 St. Valentine's Day Massacre

This new museum aims to demystify the gangsters who fought for control of Las Vegas in its early days, and the lawmen who eventually defeated them. It occupies three floors of the former Courthouse and Post Office in Downtown.

Historic site Here, in 1950, the Senate Special Committee held one of a series of nationwide hearings investigating the activities of organized crime. They found that the Capone Syndicate and New York Syndicate had turned organized crime into big business. The conclusions sent shock waves around the US, leading to the downfall of these infamous syndicates. The Mob Museum focuses on these historic events and re-creates real scenes involving the major players on both sides of the law.

Clockwise from left: Bringing Down the Mob focuses on the methods used to check on the Mob; outside The Mob Museum; Mob Mayhem highlights the violence that became a way of life; The Skim explains how money was diverted from the casinos to subsidize crime

TOP 25

Skims and mayhem There are three main sections to the museum, also known as the Las Vegas Museum of Organized Crime and Law Enforcement: Mob Mayhem, The Skim and Bringing Down the Mob. Mob Mayhem displays weapons used by mob hit men in their grisly deeds, set against a backdrop of the Museum's iconic artifact—the wall from Chicago's St. Valentine's Day Massacre. The Skim shows how the casinos' profits were "skimmed off" and sent to crime syndicates' dens. Bringing Down the Mob focuses on wiretapping—one of the most important tools used to prosecute organized crime cases. Interactive exhibits allow you to listen in on and interpret coded conversations, examine photos and surveillance films, take part in a weapons training exercise and learn about witness protection programs.

THE BASICS

www.themobmuseum.org

G2

300 Stewart Avenue, Downtown

702/229-6581

Opening early 2012; check website for details

207

HIGHLIGHTS

- The Roller Coaster
- Statue of Liberty
- Brooklyn Bridge
- Tribute to 9/11 heroes

See the sights of the Big Apple in a fraction of the time you would need to explore the real thing. The Statue of Liberty, Brookyn Bridge, the Chrysler Building—they are all here.

New York in miniature This resort hotel depicts the New York skyline through scaled-down replicas—about one-third of the actual size—of famous city landmarks. The Statue of Liberty sits side by side with skyscrapers such as the Empire State Building and a 300ft-long (91m) version of the Brooklyn Bridge. At the base of the Statue of Liberty replica is a tribute to the 9/11 heroes. Among the cherished items on display are T-shirts bearing fire station and police department insignia, and letters from firefighters.

Clockwise from far left: The nail-biting Roller Coaster; re-creations of the Empire State Building and Statue of Liberty; a replica of the New York skyline; there are plenty of places to stop for a break; hang on to your stomach!

White-knuckle ride A thrilling roller coaster twists, loops and dives at speeds of up to 67mph (108kph) around the skyscrapers to a height of 203ft (62m). Your whole world literally turns upside down and inside out when the train drops 144ft (44m). This ride was the first ever to introduce the "heartline" twist and dive move, where riders experience weightlessness—the train rolls 180 degrees, suspending its passengers 86ft (26m) above the casino roof, before taking a sudden and stomach-churning dive.

Behind the scenes The hotel's art deco lobby is set against representations of Times Square, Little Italy and Wall Street, and the casino is modeled on Central Park. A selection of restaurants and shops also follows the theme.

THE BASICS

www.nynyhotelcasino.com
🕂 D10
✉ 3790 Las Vegas Boulevard South
☎ 702/740-6969
🕐 The Roller Coaster: daily 10.30am–midnight
🍴 Several cafés and restaurants
🚇 MGM Grand
🚌 Deuce
🎡 The Roller Coaster: moderate
❓ You must be 54in (1.38m) to ride The Roller Coaster

HIGHLIGHTS

● Views from the Eiffel
Tower Observation Deck
● Shopping at Le
Boulevard

Striving to capture the Parisian style of the most elegant of European cities, this hotel has succeeded in creating fine likenesses of the Eiffel Tower, Arc de Triomphe, Paris Opera House and the Louvre.

Joie de vivre This eye-catching resort may not be the real thing, but a characteristic exuberance is reflected in little touches like singing breadmen on bikes dressed in striped shirts and berets, and a joyful "Bonjour!" from roving street performers.

Eiffel Tower Experience The symbol of this hotel is the 525ft (160m) Eiffel Tower (half the size of the original), which was re-created using Gustav Eiffel's blueprints. A glass elevator takes you to the observation deck on the 50th floor

Clockwise from far left: Replicas of the Eiffel Tower and Fontaine des Mers; neon lights; roulette table in the casino; the Eiffel Tower stands out on The Strip; the elegant lobby; experience a taste of France at Le Boulevard

for spectacular views of Las Vegas and the surrounding mountains—impressive at dusk when The Strip lights up and a prime lookout for the Bellagio fountain display opposite (▷ 16–17). Eleven floors above is the sophisticated and pricey Eiffel Tower Restaurant.

Le Boulevard Don't miss this French-style shopping boulevard, which gives you a taste of one of Europe's most lively cities. The retail space connects Paris Las Vegas to Bally's (▷ 154), the resort's sister property. Amid winding alleyways and cobbled streets, the ornate facades conceal elegant French shops, boutiques and restaurants. Weathered brickwork and brass lamps give an authentic finish, and window boxes overflowing with bright blooms complete the Parisian picture.

THE BASICS

www.parislasvegas.com

✚ D9

✉ 3655 Las Vegas Boulevard South

☎ 702/946-7000

⊛ Eiffel Tower Experience: daily 10am–1am (weather permitting)

🍴 Several cafés and restaurants

🚆 Bally's/Paris

🚌 Deuce

♿ Eiffel Tower Experience: moderate

HIGHLIGHTS

● The rainstorm outside Merchant's Harbor Coffee House
● The Miracle Mile shopping mall

Planet Hollywood, formerly the Aladdin, has made the transition from a Middle Eastern-themed hotel to the bright streets of glitzy Hollywood.

Just like Times Square Massive LED signs with continually flashing images certainly spark up this part of The Strip, and when you step inside the Planet, as it's known, you will find an even more dramatic scene of highly polished black-granite floors and a color-shifting backdrop.

Shopping with a difference Make no mistake, Miracle Mile is a shopping mall, with 170 popular international retailers, many eateries and a plethora of entertainment venues, but it couldn't be farther from just an ordinary retail

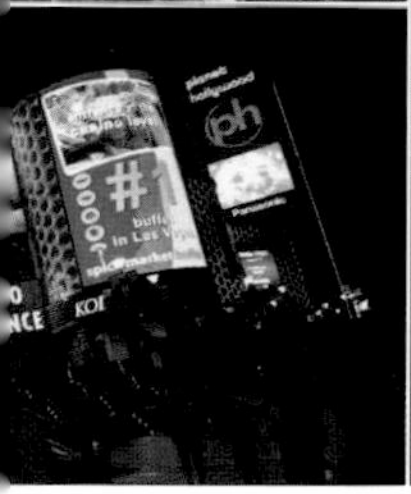

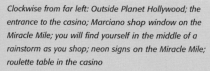

Clockwise from far left: Outside Planet Hollywood; the entrance to the casino; Marciano shop window on the Miracle Mile; you will find yourself in the middle of a rainstorm as you shop; neon signs on the Miracle Mile; roulette table in the casino

experience. Very snazzy, it has a silver grid ceiling painted with fluffy clouds and a blue sky which darkens during the day to complete the virtual reality effect. Check out the latest performances that take place at the V Theater (▷ 135). Shoppers can pause to view the multi-sensory laser show that plays hourly at the south entrance.

Stormy weather Miracle Mile is home to the bustling Merchant's Harbor, complete with the sounds of lapping waves and deckhands rushing back and forth from the freighter moored on the dockside. At intervals you will hear the rumble of distant thunder as a storm begins to brew. Clouds gather and gentle rain falls on the harbor, although you won't need an umbrella from your viewpoint on the shore.

THE BASICS

www.planethollywoodresort.com
D9
3667 Las Vegas Boulevard South
702/785-5555
Miracle Mile: Sun–Thu 9am–11pm, Fri–Sat 9am–midnight; rainstorm every hour Mon–Thu, every half hour Fri–Sun
Several cafés and restaurants
Bally's/Paris
Deuce

This canyon was created 65 million years ago when the Keystone Thrust Fault pushed one rock plate up over another. The resulting formations, in gray limestone and red sandstone, are awesome.

Focal point It's incredible to think that this striking canyon, set in the 197,000-acre (79,725ha) Red Rock Canyon National Conservation Area, is a mere 20-minute drive from the razzmatazz of Vegas. The focal point is the steep red rock escarpment, more than 13 miles (21km) long and almost 3,000ft (915m) high. More canyons have been gouged out within the formation by constant snowmelt and rains, creating the present dramatic landscape. In contrast to the dry desert, springs and streams encourage lush vegetation.

Spectacular red sandstone and gray limestone formations, along with a variety of desert vegetation, such as the Joshua tree, are distinctive features of Red Rock Canyon

Planning ahead The best place to start is at the Red Rock Visitor Center, which offers information and interpretation about all the recreational opportunities available, including horseback riding, hiking and climbing. It also has a recorded self-guide tour with a description of the geology and wildlife (all protected) in the area, and provides maps of hiking and bicycle trails and details of picnic sites. Park rangers are also on hand to give advice. Climbing should be undertaken only by experts with the correct equipment. Stick to the trails and be aware of weather conditions—flash floods do occur.

Loop the loop The 13-mile (21km) one-way Scenic Drive, leaving from the Visitor Center, lets you see some of the best rock formations and take photos at the Calico Vista viewpoints.

THE BASICS

www.nv.blm.gov/
redrockcanyon
➕ Off map at A2
✉ South Nevada,
20 miles (32km) west of
Las Vegas
☎ Red Rock Visitor
Center: 702/515-5350
🕐 Red Rock Visitor
Center: daily 8–4.30
🅿 Parking: inexpensive;
free for hikers. Scenic
Drive: inexpensive for
one-day pass

HIGHLIGHTS

- Sharks up to 12ft (3.5m) in length
- Reef Tunnel
- Talking to the naturalists
- Touch Pool
- Golden crocodiles

TIP

- Naturalist staff are available around the pathways to help answer your questions.

Fifteen different species of shark, plus 85 other magnificent aquatic species can be encountered close up in the imaginatively re-created marine environments of this excellent aquarium.

Massive tanks Shark Reef covers more than 91,000sq ft (8,450sq m) and its tanks—arranged in 14 main exhibits—contain an incredible 1.6 million gallons (7.2 million liters) of mineral-rich reconstituted sea water. It is home to more than 2,000 marine creatures—not only the sharks, but also sea turtles, reptiles and fish.

The major exhibits In Treasure Bay, a sunken ship sits on the bed of a lagoon, circled by four kinds of shark. Shoals of snapper and jack dart

Clockwise from far left: Walking through the impressive Reef Tunnel; getting up close and personal in the touch pool; a sandtiger shark; a rare shark ray; the golden crocodile is a hybrid between a saltwater and Siamese crocodile

around, in contrast to the laid-back gliding of the two green sea turtles. The experience of diving on a coral reef is re-created in the Reef Tunnel, whose water is full of bright tropical fish to the left, right and above you, and there is every probability of coming nose to nose with gray reef sharks. Elsewhere, you will see rays skimming through the water or resting on the "ocean" floor.

Reptiles, amphibians and jungle flora Rare golden crocodiles can be found in the Crocodile Habitat (the only place in the western hemisphere where you can see them), and in the Touch Pool you can get hands-on with stingrays and the prehistoric-looking horseshoe crabs. The Temple exhibits offer a refreshing rain-forest experience.

THE BASICS

www.sharkreef.com

➕ C11

✉ Mandalay Bay, 3950 Las Vegas Boulevard South

☎ 702/632-4555

🕐 Sun–Thu 10–8, Fri–Sat 10–10

🍴 Cafés and restaurants at Mandalay Bay

🚇 MGM Grand

🚌 Deuce

♿ Moderate

TOP 25

HIGHLIGHTS

● The view from the observation deck
● A gourmet meal in the Top of the World restaurant
● The thrill rides

If zooming up the tallest free-standing observation tower in the United States isn't exciting enough for you, the highest thrill rides in the world await you at the top, along with a revolving gourmet restaurant and breathtaking views.

On top of the world Marking the northern end of The Strip, the Stratosphere stands in the shadow of its 1,149ft (350m) tower, which is the main attraction. By means of speedy double-decker elevators, you can be at the five-floor complex known as the pod, which starts at 832ft (254m), in less than 30 seconds and enjoy spectacular views from the indoor observation lounge or the open-air deck. Beneath this is the revolving Top of the World gourmet restaurant (▷ 149).

Clockwise from far left: The Stratosphere Tower is an impressive piece of modern architecture; a nighttime ride on Insanity; try not to scream as X-Scream takes you over the edge; the tower is the tallest free-standing tower in the US west of the Mississippi; taking the Sky Jump

THE BASICS

www.stratospherehotel.com

➕ E5–F5

✉ 2000 Las Vegas Boulevard South

☎ 702/380-7777

🕐 Rides: Sun–Thu 11am–1am, Fri–Sat 11am–2am (hours vary seasonally)

🍴 Top of the World restaurant; cafés and restaurants

🚇 Sahara

🚌 Deuce

💵 Tower: moderate (no charge if you have a restaurant reservation). Individual rides, including admission to tower: moderate. Multiride ticket: expensive

❓ You must be at least 48in (1.22m) tall to ride the Big Shot, and 54in (1.38m) to ride X-Scream and Insanity

High-level thrills, low-level fun Attractions at the top of the tower are not for anyone who suffers from vertigo. Big Shot, 921ft (281m) high, propels you upward at 45mph (72kph), creating a G-force of four, then plummets at zero gravity. X-Scream dangles you off the side of the building, shooting you out in a small car 27ft (8m) over the edge of the tower, some 866ft (264m) above the ground, while Insanity is the ultimate in thrill rides—you experience centrifugal forces of three Gs while being spun out 64ft (19m) beyond the edge of the tower, 900ft (274m) up. Sky Jump, the latest thrill challenge, is an 855ft (261m) bungee jump from the tower—the highest controlled fall in the world. Alternatively, visit the Tower Shops, featuring themed streets reminiscent of Paris, New York and Hong Kong.

HIGHLIGHTS

● St. Mark's Square
● Grand Canal
● Street entertainers
● Grand Canal Shoppes
● Madame Tussaud's
Celebrity Encounter

TIPS

● Reservations for gondola rides must be made in person on the same day.
● You will have to walk a lot to see the whole complex; wear comfortable shoes.

Owner Sheldon Adelson's replica of Venice has gone a long way to catch the flavor of this most romantic city. But at the same time it has retained all the glitz and pizzazz expected from Las Vegas.

Most authentic This $1.5 billion resort is one of the city's most aesthetically pleasing properties. The ornate lobby has domed and vaulted ceilings, exquisite marble floors and reproductions of frescoes framed in gold. An excellent take on Venice, it has its own 1,200ft-long (365m) Grand Canal—the real one extends 2.5 miles (4km). The waterway meanders under arched bridges, including the Rialto, and past the vibrant piazza of St. Mark's Square where living statues amaze visitors with their immovable poses. In the casino hang the

Clockwise from far left: A replica of Venice's Grand Canal runs past the Grand Canal Shoppes; Enoteca San Marco in the piazza of the Grand Canal Shoppes; The Venetian at night; masterpieces adorn the ceiling of the casino; taking a romantic gondola ride on the Grand Canal

replica works of artists Tiepolo, Tintoretto and Titian. The Venetian is also home to Madame Tussaud's interactive wax museum (▷ 40–41).

Gondola ride From St. Mark's you can board a gondola and be carried down the Grand Canal to the soothing sound of water lapping against the sides; there is even a wedding gondola. Everything looks particularly spectacular at dusk, when the spirit of Venice is really captured.

Time to shop The Grand Canal Shoppes mall (▷ 119) lines an indoor cobblestoned plaza alongside the canal and is linked by walkways. There are fine restaurants and interesting shops behind faux facades, where strolling opera singers perform Italian arias and various other street entertainers do their thing.

THE BASICS

www.venetian.com

🚇 D8

✉ 3355 Las Vegas Boulevard South

☎ 702/414-1000. Grand Canal Shoppes/gondola ride: 702/414-4500

🕐 Gondola ride: Sun–Thu 10am–11pm, Fri–Sat 10am–midnight; last ride 15 min before closing

🍴 Cafés and restaurants

🚉 Harrah's/Imperial Palace

🚌 Deuce

🎡 Gondola ride: moderate

24 Wedding Chapels

Whether your ideal wedding is being married by Elvis, tying the knot in a hot-air balloon, going for the quick drive-through ceremony or just a traditional approach, Vegas will have a chapel that can oblige.

What your heart desires Many hotels have elegant wedding chapels, or you can opt for an outdoor location amid majestic Nevada mountains and canyons. Anything goes in Las Vegas. If you're going to the chapel and you're going to get married, then some of the chapels north of Sahara Avenue will provide a day to remember. Passing visitors are also welcome.

Gathered together in the sight of Elvis The Graceland Wedding Chapel and Viva Las Vegas Wedding Chapel offer the most renowned style

Clockwise from far left: Just one of the wedding themes on offer at the Viva Las Vegas Wedding Chapel; the Little White Wedding Chapel; an Elvis lookalike sings at a wedding; rent a stretch limo and arrive in style; Viva Las Vegas Wedding Chapel's famous pink Cadillac

of wedding in Las Vegas, the one that's conducted by an Elvis look-alike. Graceland (▷ 69) is small, offering a more intimate experience, while Viva Las Vegas has options, such as riding into the chapel in a pink Cadillac.

Chapel of the Bells Follow in the footsteps of actor Mickey Rooney and football legend Pelé in this most polished of venues. Among their promotions are a free bottle of champagne and personalized wedding certificate.

Little White Wedding Chapel The setting of many celebrity weddings (including one of Joan Collins' marriages), with traditional ceremonies around the clock—simply show up and wait your turn. The Little White Chapel in the Sky marries couples in a hot-air balloon.

THE BASICS

Viva Las Vegas Wedding Chapel
www.vivalasvegas.com
⊞ F4
✉ 1205 Las Vegas Boulevard South
☎ 702/384-0771

Chapel of the Bells
www.chapelofthebells lasvegas.com
⊞ F5
✉ 2233 Las Vegas Boulevard South
☎ 702/735-6803

Little White Wedding Chapel
www.littlewhitechapel.com
⊞ F4
✉ 1301 Las Vegas Boulevard South
☎ 702/382-5943

25 Wynn Las Vegas

HIGHLIGHTS

- Waterfall and lagoon
- Lake of Dreams show
- Art collection
- Ferrari-Maserati showroom
- Le Rêve show

This $2.7 billion resort opened in 2005, a stunning creation by Las Vegas entrepreneur and developer Steve Wynn. If you can't afford to stay here, there's nothing to stop you gazing at its magnificence.

Dazzling splendor This incredible showpiece covers 215 acres (87ha) and is one of the tallest buildings in Vegas, towering 60 stories over The Strip. The grounds are an evergreen oasis with trickling streams, the scent of fresh flowers and an integrated 18-hole golf course (open to guests only).

Spectacles for free A lagoon backed by a 150ft (46m) man-made mountain, complete with waterfall, takes center stage. A visual spectacular, the Lake of Dreams, is projected

Clockwise from far left: Parasol Down lobby bar; the Wynn Las Vegas and its sister property, the Encore, behind; Wynn Las Vegas towers 60 stories above The Strip; shopping on Wynn Esplanade; the spectacular Lake of Dreams light show

onto the water and a screen that rises out of the lagoon. Window-shop on Wynn Esplanade (▷ 123), with its collection of designer shops, and visit the full-size Ferrari-Maserati dealership, where some of the most yearned-after cars in the world are displayed. Steve Wynn's personal art collection is kept here too, in the executive offices; it includes works by Matisse, Renoir and Rembrandt, and most significantly Pablo Picasso's *Le Rêve*, purchased by Wynn in 1997 for $48.4 million.

Sensational performance For a memorable experience, try not to miss the Le Rêve spectacular—an aquatic show in an aqua theater-in-the-round that dazzles with its extraordinary acrobatic feats, amazing sound-and-light effects and superb choreography.

THE BASICS

www.wynnlasvegas.com

➕ D7–E7

✉ 3131 Las Vegas Boulevard South

☎ 702/770-7000

🕐 Lake of Dreams at regular intervals during the day and evening; Le Rêve: Fri–Tue 7 and 9.30pm

🍴 Several restaurants and cafés

🚇 Harrah's/Imperial Palace

🚌 Deuce

👜 Waterfall show free; Le Rêve very expensive

More to See

This section contains other great places to visit if you have more time. Some are in the heart of the city while others are a short journey away, found under Further Afield. This chapter also has fantastic excursions that you should set aside a whole day to visit.

MORE TO SEE

In the Heart of the City

THE ARTS FACTORY
www.theartsfactory.com
At this complex in the heart of the 18b Las Vegas Arts District, talented local artists are showcased across some 25 galleries and studios. This is the main venue for First Friday, which is held on the first Friday of each month. Galleries stay open late (6–10pm), artists display their work and street bands perform.
🔲 F4 ✉ 107 East Charleston Boulevard
☎ 702/383-3133 🕐 Times vary; some areas are closed to the public. Bar and bistro: Tue–Fri 11–3, Tue–Sat 5–10pm 🚌 Deuce; free bus service between First Friday stops
✋ Free

ATOMIC TESTING MUSEUM
www.atomictestingmuseum.org
Opened in February 2005, this is the first museum of its kind in the US and provides an interesting insight into the work of the Nevada Test Site and its impact. Three miles (5km) from The Strip, the museum is certainly something different and a long way from the superficial hype of Las Vegas.

Interactive exhibits help you learn about the history of nuclear power, and you can experience a simulated atomic explosion in the Ground Zero Theater.
🔲 F9 ✉ 755 East Flamingo Road
☎ 702/794-5124 🕐 Mon–Sat 10–5, Sun 12–5 🚌 202 ✋ Moderate

THE BEATLES: LOVE
www.themirage.com
Another Cirque du Soleil production, LOVE celebrates the musical legacy of The Beatles and explores their songs in a series of scenes inhabited by real and imaginary people. It's staged in a purpose-built circular theater.
🔲 D8 ✉ The Mirage, 3400 Las Vegas Boulevard South ☎ 702/792-7777
🕐 Thu–Mon 7 and 9.30pm 🚉 Harrah's/Imperial Palace 🚌 Deuce ✋ Very expensive

BELLAGIO GALLERY OF FINE ART
www.bellagio.com
The first gallery on The Strip shows a serious side to Las Vegas culture. The facility is a non-commercial

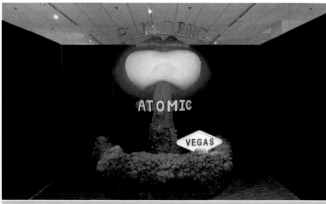
Building Atomic Vegas at the Atomic Testing Museum

venue that showcases two high-quality art exhibitions per year from major museums across the US and beyond.

🔀 D9 ✉ Bellagio, 3600 Las Vegas Boulevard South ☎ 702/693-7871 🕐 Sun–Tue, Thu 10–6, Wed, Fri–Sat 10–7; last admission 30 min before closing 🚌 Bally's/Paris 🚍 Deuce 💷 Moderate

CSI: THE EXPERIENCE
www.mgmgrand.com
Based on the hit TV series, here you can choose from four grisly crimes and follow clues in reconstructed scenes to discover if you make the grade as a sleuth.

🔀 D10 ✉ MGM Grand, 3799 Las Vegas Boulevard South ☎ 702/891-1111 🕐 Daily 10–10 🚌 MGM Grand 🚍 Deuce 💷 Expensive

FASHION SHOW MALL
www.thefashionshow.com
Following a huge $362 million expansion, this mall is one of the country's largest and the city's premier retail destination. It is anchored by popular department stores Macy's (▷ 120) and

Neiman Marcus, and the structure enclosing the mall is known as the Cloud, acting as shade during the day and a movie screen at night.

🔀 D7 ✉ 3200 Las Vegas Boulevard South ☎ 702/784-7000 🕐 Mon–Sat 10–9, Sun 11–7 🍴 Numerous restaurants and cafés 🚌 Harrah's/Imperial Palace 🚍 Deuce

FLAMINGO WILDLIFE HABITAT
www.flamingolasvegas.com
A lush 15-acre (6ha) paradise has been re-created at the Flamingo to provide a home to more than 300 exotic birds, including flamingos and penguins.

🔀 D9 ✉ Flamingo, 3555 Las Vegas Boulevard South ☎ 702/733-3111 🕐 Daily 24 hours 🚌 Flamingo/Caesars 🚍 Deuce 💷 Free

FLIGHTLINEZ
http://fremontstreetflightline.com
Whiz along a high zip line at speeds of up to 30mph (48kph), suspended beneath the Fremont Street canopy roof. Flightlinez is a fun new attraction that adds an action thrill dimension to Downtown's busiest tourism hub.

An oasis of calm at Flamingo Wildlife Habitat

Fashion show at the Fashion Show Mall

🚩 G3 ✉ 425 Fremont Street (next to Walgreens) ☎ 702/739-2222 ◎ Mon–Thu 2pm–midnight, Fri–Sun 2pm–2am 🚌 107, Deuce 💷 Moderate; all-day pass expensive

FOUR SEASONS SPA
www.fourseasons.com/lasvegas
An exquisite facility for the ultimate in pampering, treatments include facials, body scrubs, massages and mud treatments, and there are two private spa suites, with sauna, steam room, whirlpool tub and massage table. The fitness suite includes cardiovascular equipment and weights, saunas and jacuzzis, and there's a jogging track through the beautiful grounds.
🚩 D11 ✉ Four Seasons, 3960 Las Vegas Boulevard South ☎ 702/632-5000 ◎ Daily 8–8 🚇 MGM Grand 🚌 Deuce

GAMEWORKS
www.gameworks.com
A creation from movie mogul Steven Spielberg that is the ultimate in interactive, virtual-reality arcade games, GameWorks is geared mostly to teenagers, though after 9pm any visitor under

18 years must be accompanied by an adult (over 21). You can pay per game (from $1) or buy timed play cards valid from one hour ($20) up to a whole day pass ($35). Food and drink are available from the fast-food counter.
🚩 D10 ✉ Showcase Mall, 3785 Las Vegas Boulevard South ☎ 702/432-4263 ◎ Sun–Thu 10am–midnight, Fri–Sat 10am–1am 🚇 MGM Grand 🚌 Deuce 💷 Admission free; individual activities inexpensive

GOLDEN NUGGET
www.goldennugget.com
One of Las Vegas's original casinos, built in 1946, the Golden Nugget was given a $300 million refurbishment between 2006 and 2009. The star attraction is The Tank—a central water feature complete with a 200,000-gallon (909,218-liter) shark tank. Slide down a transparent tube through the middle of the tank to get a closer view of its residents.
🚩 G3 ✉ 129 East Fremont Street ☎ 702/385-7111 ◎ Daily 24 hours. Tank: daily 10–10 🚌 108, Deuce

Video arcade in GameWorks, in the Showcase Mall

GRACELAND WEDDING CHAPEL

www.gracelandchapel.com

Graceland, one of the city's best-known wedding chapels, has been joining happy couples for more than 50 years. Celebrities who have tied the knot here include Jon Bon Jovi, Cameron Diaz and Johnny Depp, as well as members of rock bands such as KISS, Deep Purple, Def Leppard and the Beastie Boys. It has become one of the many Elvis "shrines," where the bride and groom can take their vows before a look-alike of the King himself. Various Elvis wedding packages are available, depending on your fanaticism and budget. Unless there is a wedding ceremony going on, you are welcome to look around the quaint little white-painted chapel, unmissable with its typically Vegas neon sign. Join one of the several guided tours (free), or wander around independently.

✚ G4 ✉ 619 Las Vegas Boulevard South ☎ 702/382-0091 🕑 Daily 8am–midnight 🚍 Deuce

JUBILEE!

www.ballyslasvegas.com

Jubilee's cast of scantily clad showgirls in massive headdresses and little else—many appear topless—remains as popular as when the show opened in 1981. Though the original concept is unchanged, brand-new routines and segments are introduced on a regular basis.

✚ D9 ✉ Jubilee Theater, Bally's, 3645 Las Vegas Boulevard South ☎ 702/946-4567 🕑 Sat–Thu 7.30pm and 10.30pm 🚉 Bally's/Paris 🚍 Deuce 💲 Very expensive ❓ Minimum age limit 18 years

LIED DISCOVERY CHILDREN'S MUSEUM

www.ldcm.org

Constantly changing exhibits introduce children to the wonders of science, communication technology and the environment. It's lots of fun, with interactive, hands-on activities, and should appeal particularly to under-5s. There are also themed displays, and fun experiments to try out in Einstein's Corner.

The Golden Nugget, off Fremont Street

Making giant bubbles at the Lied Discovery Children's Museum

H2 ✉ 833 Las Vegas Boulevard North
☎ 702/382-3445 🕐 Tue–Fri 9–4, Sat 10–5,
Sun 12–5 🚌 113 💵 Inexpensive

M&M'S WORLD
www.m-ms.com
An interactive retail complex over
four floors with M&M's brand
merchandise items, plus a 3-D
movie theater, an M&M's Racing
Team store and a wall covered in
colored plain and peanut M&Ms.
D10 ✉ Showcase Mall, 3785 Las Vegas
Boulevard South ☎ 702/736-7611
🕐 Daily 9am–midnight 🚊 MGM Grand
🚌 Deuce 💵 Admission and movie free

MARJORIE BARRICK MUSEUM OF NATURAL HISTORY
http://barrickmuseum.unlv.edu
Less than 3 miles (5km) from
The Strip, on the UNLV university
campus, is this excellent museum
devoted to the Native Americans
of the region, the wildlife and also
the history of Mesoamerica from
2000BC to the present.
G10 ✉ 4505 South Maryland Parkway
☎ 702/895-3381 🕐 Mon–Fri 8–4.45, Sat
10–2 🚌 109 💵 Free–donation

MENOPAUSE: THE MUSICAL
www.luxor.com
This comedy musical is hilarious
with a heart, following three
women as they come to terms
with entering "the change" in their
lives. It's a fast-paced show, with
no taboo topic untouched, but is
compassionate and sensitive.
D11 ✉ Atrium Showroom, Luxor,
3900 Las Vegas Boulevard South
☎ 702/262-4400 🕐 Wed–Mon 5.30pm,
Tue 8pm 🚊 MGM Grand 🚌 Deuce
💵 Very expensive

THE MOB EXPERIENCE
www.lvme.com
At the back of the Tropicana is this
fun new interactive exhibition,
offering visitors a personalized tour
through the murky underworld of
organized crime. Led by Godfather
actor James Caan on video
screens and 3-D holograms, you
make your way through dark alleys
and illicit dens, following a series
of challenges to test your honesty.
Offered a wad of ill-gotten cash, do
you pass it on to the Mob, or hand
it over to law officers? If, by the

*Exhibit at the Marjorie Barrick
Museum of Natural History
M&M's World, home of
the popular candy*

end, you have failed the test, you could be gunned down in a hail of simulated bullets! Also on display are some 1,000 items of Mob memorabilia and historic artifacts, including Meyer Lansky's diary and one of Bugsy Siegel's cars.

➕ D10 ✉ 3801 Las Vegas Boulevard South ☎ 702/739-2222 ⏱ Daily 10–10 🚇 MGM Grand 🚌 Deuce, 201 💰 Expensive

MONTE CARLO

www.montecarlo.com

Chandeliered domes, ornate fountains and gaslit promenades set the scene at this resort hotel, modeled on the Place du Casino in Monte Carlo. There are several lively restaurants, including Diablo's Cantina, whose giant "Wheel O'Sin" adds an extra gambling dimension to cocktail happy hour. The eclectic entertainment includes Jabbawockeez stage spectacle, and rubber-faced impressionist Frank Caliendo.

➕ D10 ✉ 3770 Las Vegas Boulevard South ☎ 702/730-7777 🚇 MGM Grand 🚌 Deuce

NATHAN BURTON COMEDY MAGIC

www.nathanburton.com

Nathan Burton is an escapologist extraordinaire whose rapid-fire tricks tend toward the wacky, slightly risqué and artfully improvised range of the genre. He hit the big time following his appearance on NBC's *America's Got Talent* TV show in 2006. Expect plenty of dry ice, scantily clad showgirls and hilariously set-up members of the audience.

➕ D9 ✉ Flamingo Showroom, Flamingo, 3555 Las Vegas Boulevard South ☎ 702/733-3333 ⏱ Tue–Sun 2pm and 4pm 🚇 Flamingo/Caesars 🚌 Deuce 💰 Expensive

NEON BONEYARD PARK

www.neonmuseum.org

Ten of the city's famed neon signs dating back to 1940 have been refurbished and displayed as installation art, on or just off Fremont Street (open 24/7). Highlights are two of Vegas's most iconic nostalgic signs, Vegas Vic and Vegas Vicki: Vic is perched on

The entrance to the Monte Carlo features an ornate arch, statues and a fountain

An old neon sign for The Flame

top of the Pioneer Club and Vicki is on the Girls of Glitter Gulch. You can take a guided tour to the Neon Boneyard Museum, a collection of vintage signs from around the city. Tours pick up from your hotel.

🚩 H2 ✉ Fremont Street ☎ 702/387-6366 ⓒ Guided tours to New Boneyard Museum: Tue–Fri 12 and 2, Sat 9.30 and 11. Advanced booking essential (minimum donation $15) 🚌 108, Deuce

NURTURE, THE SPA AT LUXOR

www.luxor.com

Soothe your tired body in beautiful surroundings. A whole range of exercise equipment—treadmills, bicycles, weight machines, climbing machines—is available here, along with such treatments as body wraps, body scrubs, massages, hydrotherapy and facials. Specialty massages include ashiatsu: foot massage from therapists hanging from ceiling bars. There are tanning beds, too.

🚩 C11 ✉ Luxor, 3900 Las Vegas Boulevard South ☎ 702/262-4000 ⓒ Daily 8am–8.30pm 🚇 MGM Grand 🚌 Deuce

OLD MORMON FORT

http://parks.nv.gov/olvmf.htm

The first people to settle the area were Mormons, who built a fort here in the mid-19th century, at a site now considered "the place where Las Vegas began." They turned to farming, but were driven out in 1858 by frequent Native American raids. The fort, which was built in 1855, has been reconstructed, with one original wall surviving. The Visitor Center tells their story with displays and historic artifacts.

🚩 H2 ✉ 500 East Washington Avenue ☎ 702/486-3511 ⓒ Tue–Sat 8–4.30 🚌 113 💷 Inexpensive

SHOW IN THE SKY

www.riolasvegas.com

It's carnival time every day at the Rio. Mardi Gras floats suspended from the ceiling parade above the casino floor and for a fee you can take a magical ride on board.

🚩 B8 ✉ Rio, 3700 West Flamingo Road ☎ 702/777-7777 ⓒ Shows Sun–Wed hourly 6–11pm 🚌 202 💷 Show free; ride moderate

History buffs will appreciate a stroll around the Old Mormon Fort

SIRENS OF TI

www.treasureisland.com

A swashbuckling battle between sexy sirens and renegade pirates takes place at Siren's Cove, at the hotel entrance. There's music, seductive dancing and plenty of loud explosions. Arrive early.

➕ D8 ✉ Treasure Island, 3300 Las Vegas Boulevard South ☎ 702/894-7111 🕐 Nightly 5.30, 7, 8.30, 10 (dependent on weather); shows last 90 min 🚉 Harrah's/Imperial Palace 🚌 Deuce 💷 Free

SPA MANDALAY

www.mandalaybay.com

This opulent facility has picture windows with a wonderful view over the hotel's lagoon and gardens. In addition to traditional treatments, there is a range of more exotic techniques, including ayurvedic relaxation and Swedish massage, while amenities include whirlpools with waterfalls, saunas and Swedish showers.

➕ D11 ✉ Mandalay Bay, 3950 Las Vegas Boulevard South ☎ 702/632-7220 🕐 Daily 6am–8.30pm 🚉 MGM Grand 🚌 Deuce

TONY N' TINA'S WEDDING

www.tonyandtinavegas.com

Considered to be one of the best and most successful Off-Broadway shows, Tony n' Tina's Wedding arrived at Planet Hollywood in 2002. This is a show with a difference. If you don't get to go to a real wedding while you are in Vegas, come here for the next best thing. Audience participation is key and everyone gets to attend the wildest and most raucous Italian-American ceremony and reception. You even get the Italian buffet, complete with wedding cake.

➕ D9 ✉ Planet Hollywood Resort, 3367 Las Vegas Boulevard South ☎ 702/785-5555 (702/949-6450 for tickets) 🕐 Mon–Sat 7pm 🚉 Bally's/Paris 🚌 Deuce 💷 Expensive

TRUMP INTERNATIONAL HOTEL

www.trumplasvegashotel.com

At 64-stories high this is the city's tallest residential building and it has exterior windows gilded in 24-carat gold. Opened 2008, it is

Members of the audience are encouraged to take part in Tony n' Tina's Wedding

The Trump International Hotel

the creation of business magnate and celebrity Donald Trump, housing a mix of hotel suites and residential condominiums. There's no casino here but the restaurant and cocktail bar, DJT (▷ 142), has a good reputation.

➕ D7 ✉ 2000 Fashion Show Drive ☎ 702/982-0000 🍽 Restaurant 🚌 Deuce

VIVA ELVIS

www.arialasvegas.com

There's a whole lotta shaking and rocking to the King's greatest hits in Cirque du Soleil's latest production, a high-tempo, high-tech homage to the life and music of Elvis. The show is a dazzling, pelvic-pulsating experience, combining dance, acrobatics and music.

➕ C10 ✉ ARIA, CityCenter, 3730 Las Vegas Boulevard South ☎ 702/590-7111 🕐 Tue–Sat 7pm and 9.30pm 🚇 Bally's/Paris 🚌 Deuce 💷 Very expensive

"WELCOME TO FABULOUS LAS VEGAS" SIGN

Designed in 1959 by Betty Willis, this famous sign welcomes you as you enter Las Vegas at the south end of The Strip. Standing on a clipped lawn and flanked by palm trees in the central freeway, the diamond-shaped neon sign is a popular photo stop on guided city tours, often with showgirls and Elvis look-alikes on hand for cheesy portraits.

➕ D12 ✉ 5200 Las Vegas Boulevard South 🚌 104, 116, Deuce

WET REPUBLIC ULTRA POOL

www.mgmgrand.com

Forget nightlife, this is the latest Vegas craze—daylife. Grab your most fashionable swimwear and visit the MGM for the ultimate pool experience. Here you will find two state-of-the-art saltwater pools, eight individual pools and spas, party cabanas and comfortable loungers. DJs spin hot beats and entertainers take the stage, while party animals dance, shmooze or cool off in the water. Let the party begin (minimum age 21).

➕ D10 ✉ MGM Grand, 3799 Las Vegas Boulevard South ☎ 702/891-3563 🕐 Daily 11am–dusk 🚇 MGM Grand 🚌 Deuce

The sign says it all

Grab your swimwear and head for Wet Republic

Further Afield

CLARK COUNTY WETLANDS PARK

www.accessclarkcounty.com/parks
Just 8 miles (13km) east of The Strip, this environmentally concious park has a visitor center where you can pick up trail maps. Bird-watching is popular here, with species that include great blue herons, snowy egrets and black-bellied whistling ducks.

➕ Off map at J10 ✉ 7050 Wetlands Park Lane ☎ 702/455-7522 ⏰ Visitor Center: daily 9–3. Nature Center: daily dawn–dusk 🚌 202, then walk 1 mile (1.5km) 💲 Free

ETHEL M. CHOCOLATE FACTORY

www.ethelm.com
Take a self-guiding audio tour to discover how Ethel Mars's chocolate enterprise began and get an insight into the production processes. To complete the visit, sample your favorite candy.

➕ Off map at J11 ✉ 2 Cactus Garden Drive, Henderson (8 miles/13km southeast of Las Vegas) ☎ 702/435-2655 ⏰ Daily 8.30–7 (hours may vary on holidays) 🚌 217 💲 Free

NEVADA STATE MUSEUM

Learn all about life before Vegas, and view exhibits of dinosaurs and early man right through to the controversial nuclear testing program. Photographic displays of Las Vegas in the early years are on show. It's scheduled to move to the Springs Preserve (▷ below) in 2012, but dates are not confirmed.

➕ B2 ✉ 700 Twin Lakes Drive ☎ 702/486-5205

SPRINGS PRESERVE

www.springspreserve.org
Springs Preserve is set in 180 acres (73ha) on the site of the original water source for Las Vegas, which dried up in 1962. Learn more about desert living through interactive displays and exhibits. There are 8 acres (3ha) of gardens and walking trails.

➕ B3 ✉ 333 South Valley View Boulevard, between US95 and Alta Drive ☎ 702/822-7700 ⏰ Daily 10–6 🍴 Springs Café 🚌 201, 202, 204 from Strip, disembark at Valley View Boulevard stop and take bus 104 north to Meadows Mall 💲 Moderate; gardens and trails free

The delightful gardens at Springs Preserve

Watching a simulated flash flood at Springs Preserve

Excursions

DEATH VALLEY

www.nps.gov/deva

This vast desert sprawls for nearly 150 miles (240km) between Las Vegas and the Pacific Coast, a few hours' drive west of the city, across the border in California. It makes for an adventurous day trip, with options for driving tours, hiking and bike rides.

It is the largest national park in the continental US, covering nearly 3.1 million acres (1.25 million ha). It is also the hottest and driest place in North America, with daytime temperatures regularly reaching 120°F (48.9°C) and rainfall averaging less than 2in (5cm) a year. It comprises a huge range of dramatic landscapes and vegetation: from its highest point at Telescope Peak, 11,049ft (3,368m) above sea level, to Badwater Basin, at 282ft (86m) below sea level—the lowest point in the Western Hemisphere. Its geological history has produced a breathtaking array of colored rock layers, carved by erosion over millennia. Some of the best panoramas are at Artist's Palette, Zabriskie Point, the Devil's Golf Course and Dante's View.

Humans settled here 10,000 years ago, and their descendents, the Timbisha Shoshone tribe, still maintain their ancestral homelands in protected areas. Others made their mark more recently, such as Death Valley Scotty, in whose memory Scotty's Castle was built in the 1920s.

Register at the Furnace Creek Visitor Center where you can pick up free maps/leaflets. These give details of hiking trails, as well as guided activities. From 2012, a new center will include an exhibition space and a museum.

Distance: 120 miles (193km) northwest of Las Vegas. From Las Vegas take Nevada State Highway 160 via Pahrump to Death Valley junction, then California State Highway 127 and 190 to Furnace Creek

Journey Time: 2 hours

✉ Furnace Creek Visitor Center, California Highway 190 ☎ 760/786-3200 🕐 Daily 8–5 🖐 Moderate

Pink Jeep Tours

☎ 702/895-6777; www.pinkjeep.com

Hiking in Death Valley

Death Valley is the hottest and driest national park in the US

GRAND CANYON

www.nps.gov/grca

To stand on the rim of the Grand Canyon and look down to its floor a mile (1.6km) below is to be confronted with raw nature at its most awe-inspiring. It's a sight from which you can never detract or tire of.

The Grand Canyon stretches some 277 miles (446km) along the Colorado River, and it is this mighty river that created it, eroding the landscape over 5 million years. This erosion has revealed layer upon twisted layer of limestone, sandstone and shale, a fascinating geological cross-section of the earth's crust. At its widest point it is 17 miles (27km) from one side to the other and its deepest point is 1 mile (1.6km) beneath the rim.

The South Rim, 260 miles (418km) from Las Vegas, is the more touristy side of the canyon, because it's more accessible, with an airport and rail depot. Grand Canyon Village here also has lots of visitor facilities, including hotels, restaurants, shops and museums.

In addition, this is the start point for treks down into the canyon; if you have the energy this is a wonderful way to appreciate the topography to the full.

Even more accessible from Vegas, only 120 miles (193km) away, is Grand Canyon West, with its famous SkyWalk. The five-layered glass platform, suspended above the canyon floor, offers amazing, heart-pounding views, from 4,000ft (1,220m) up.

Distance: South Rim 260 miles (418km) from Las Vegas; Grand Canyon West 120 miles (193km) from Las Vegas

Journey Time: 3.5 hours to South Rim; 2.5 hours to Grand Canyon West

✉ South Rim Visitor Center: opposite Mather Point (about 4 miles/6.5km north of the south entrance station). Grand Canyon West is at the end of Diamond Bar Road, beyond Dolan Springs, off US93, 40 miles (64km) from Hoover Dam 🕒 South Rim Visitor Center: daily 8–5 (longer during peak times). SkyWalk: Apr–Sep daily 7–7; Oct–Mar 8–5 💲 SkyWalk: expensive 🛈 It is best to take an organized tour. Many companies offer bus, helicopter and light aircraft trips from Las Vegas

The glass-bottomed SkyWalk at the West Rim of the Grand Canyon

Looking out over the canyon from the South Rim

MOUNT CHARLESTON

www.fs.usda.gov/htnf

Only a short drive away and always cooler than Las Vegas—by as much as 40°F (22°C)—this lovely alpine wilderness is a joy to visit.

Located in the forested Spring Mountains, some 35 miles (56km) northwest of Las Vegas, Charleston's peak reaches 11,900ft (3,628m). It is snowcapped for more than half the year, and is sometimes even visible from The Strip. Its official name is the Spring Mountains National Recreation Area, which forms part of the surrounding Humboldt-Toiyabe National Forest. Charleston and its surrounding countryside are popular for their plentiful activities, including hiking (51 miles/82km of trails), horseback riding, mountain biking, rock climbing, picnicking and camping. During winter months, the US Forest Service runs various organized activities, including guided snowshoe hikes during winter weekends. There are campsites with full facilities, as well as picnic areas with hookups for RVs (caravans) and trailers.

Nearby Lee Canyon is a great spot for winter sports, including cross-country skiing and snowshoeing. When there is enough snow, horse-drawn sleigh rides leave from here (Robert Humphrey's Trail Rides, tel 702/596-6715). Thick bristlecone pines cling to the limestone cliffs forming an awesome backdrop. The US Forest Service maintains the marked trails, which are suitable for all abilities. At the top of Kyle Canyon, Mount Charleston Lodge offers comfortable log-cabin accommodation, good food and live entertainment in front of an open fire, with breathtaking views (http://mtcharlestonlodge.com).

Distance: 35 miles (56km) northwest of Las Vegas

Journey Time: 30 min

☎ 702/515-5400 ⚡ Take an organized tour or go by car (check road conditions in winter). From Las Vegas, take I-15 west and continue to US95 north. Stay on US95 until Kyle Canyon Road, then follow signs to Mount Charleston

Mount Charleston Lodge

Snow-capped Mount Charleston in the Spring Mountain Range

VALLEY OF FIRE STATE PARK

www.parks.nv.gov/vf.htm

Nevada's first state park takes its name from its red sandstone rock formations, formed more than 150 million years ago by a shift in the earth's crust and eroded by water and wind. The resulting weird and wonderful shapes resemble everything from elephants to pianos. You might also be lucky enough to spot tree stumps that have survived from an ancient 250-million-year-old forest.

Note the ancient rock art (petroglyphs) by the prehistoric Basketmaker people and Anasazi Pueblo farmers, who lived along the Muddy River between 300BC and AD1150, and who are thought to be North America's earliest inhabitants. Petroglyphs created by these people can be seen on rocks in several sites dotted around the park, including Atlatl Rock (ask for information at the visitor center). Geological highlights include petrified logs, and weird sandstone formations created by erosion from wind and water, some of the best examples of which can be seen at Arch Rock and the Beehives. Exotic wildlife living here includes roadrunners, coyotes, lizards, snakes, antelope, ground squirrels and rare desert tortoises.

You can hike along the park's well-marked trails, or enjoy its other activities, such as rock hunting, camping and picnicking. The visitor center provides information and trail maps. A short scenic drive from here goes up to the Rainbow Vista, a lookout point with great views of some of the park's most impressive colored rockscapes.

Not far from the Valley of Fire is Lake Mead (▷ 33), which, with its water-sports activities and fishing opportunities, makes a good combination for a day trip.

Distance: 55 miles (88km) northeast of Las Vegas

Journey Time: 1 hour

✉ Visitor Center: SR169 in Overton
☎ 702/397-2088 🕐 Daily 8.30–4.30
🅿 Parking inexpensive ❓ Take an organized tour or go by car via I-15 from Las Vegas

Rock formation caused by the erosion of wind and water

Petroglyph Canyon is famous for its ancient rock art

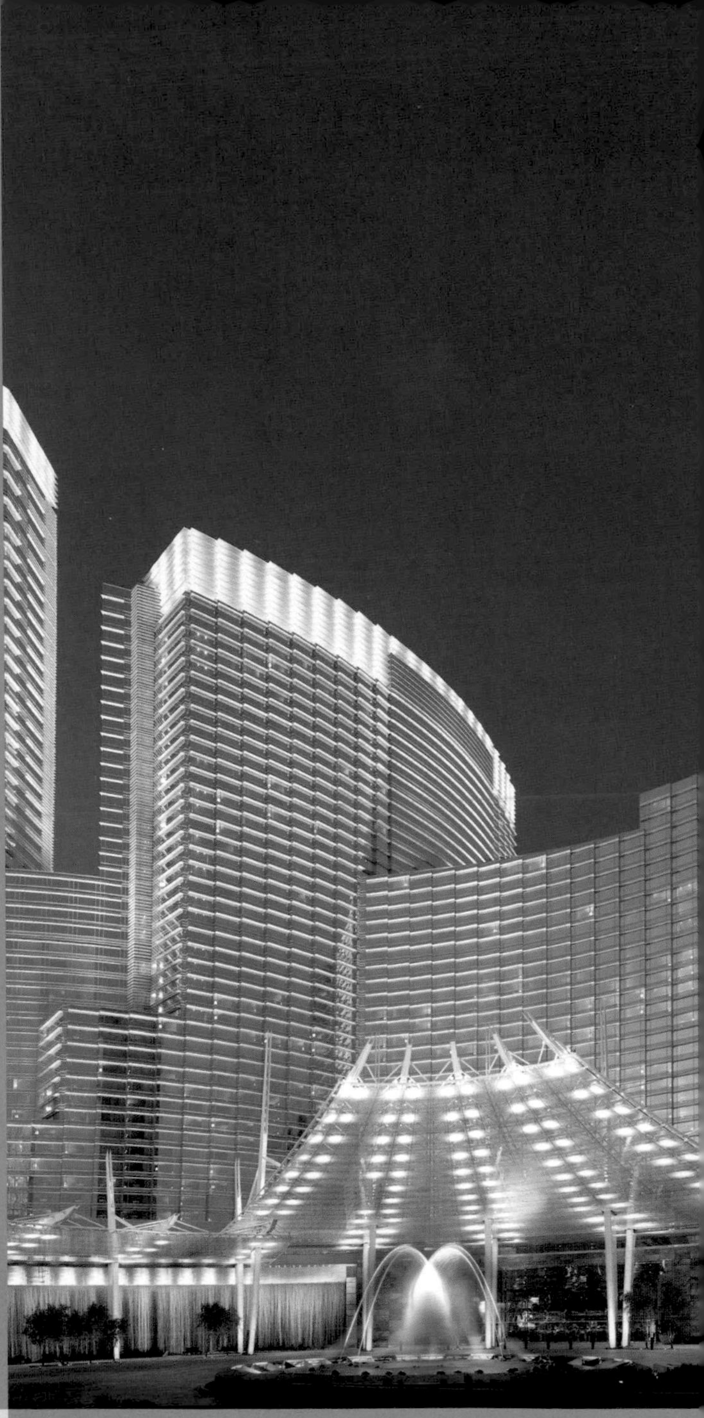

City Tours

This section contains self-guided tours that will help you explore the sights in each of the city's regions. Each tour is designed to take a day, with a map pinpointing the recommended places along the way. There is a quick reference guide at the end of each tour, listing everything you need in that region, so you know exactly what's close by.

South Strip

Expect a thrilling day of wildlife spectacle, cultural wonders and white-knuckle rides. The spacious South Strip also offers some of the city's most adventurous architecture and global cuisine; from New York-New York to Luxor and Mandalay Bay, you can eat your way around the world.

Morning
Start at the Tropicana to visit its new **Mob Experience** interactive museum (▷ 70–71), where you can discover your inner criminal tendencies! Cross the overhead walkway over Tropicana Avenue East to the MGM Grand, guarded outside by the MGM Lion statue, with the real kings of the jungle on show inside in the **Lion Habitat** (▷ 36–37).

Lunch
Cross the walkway over The Strip to **New York-New York** (▷ 46–47). Ride The Roller Coaster around its nearly life-size skyscrapers. Have lunch at **Il Fornaio Panetteria** (▷ 143) Italian bakery and café.

Afternoon
Cross the walkway over Tropicana Avenue to see **Excalibur's** (▷ 28–29) medieval fantasy towers. Inside this multicolored castle you enter the Medieval Village. Mingle with costumed performers, dodge the fiery breath of the dragon, and have fun with traditional carnival attractions, more up-to-date high-tech games or simulator rides.

Mid-afternoon

Leaving Excalibur, take a short bus ride just down The Strip to **Luxor** (▷ 38–39), one of the city's most striking architectural monuments, fronted by the Sphinx. The *Titanic* and Bodies exhibitions are an odd combination to find inside a life-size Egyptian pyramid, some might think, but both are hugely popular and moving in different ways. In *Titanic* you can touch a giant block of ice to help you imagine how the passengers might have felt as this huge liner sank, while Bodies…The Exhibition shows you the workings of actual dissected and preserved human bodies.

Late afternoon

Turn right out of Luxor and take the monorail down to Mandalay Bay, to visit the **Shark Reef** (▷ 54–55) aquarium inside the convention center behind the hotel. This conservation-oriented feature is arranged in different habitats, with many colorful species of fish and reptiles on show, as well as 15 different types of shark. You can even immerse yourself in the experience, entering an underwater glass tunnel, from which you can watch the fish swimming over and around you.

Evening

Have dinner at **Fleur** (▷ 143), celebrity chef Hubert Keller's superb new gastro-tapas restaurant inside the Mandalay Bay hotel. Soothe your aching limbs at **Spa Mandalay** (▷ 73) and round off your evening with a short taxi ride down The Strip to see the iconic **"Welcome to Fabulous Las Vegas" sign** (▷ 74). The diamond-shaped neon sign standing in the central reservation marks the start of The Strip.

⑧

The Beatles:
LOVE

Harrah's

Harrah's/
Imperial Palace

Westchester Drive

Ida Avenue

Spa at
Caesars

The Auto
Collections

Winnick Avenue

Albert Avenue

EXIT 38

Caesars Palace
& the Forum

Nathan Burton
Comedy Magic

Flamingo Wildlife
Habitat

Flamingo

Flamingo/
Caesars Palace

Flamingo Road East

Jubilee!

Bellagio
Gallery of
Fine Art

Bally's

Paris
Las Vegas

Bally's/
Paris Las Vegas

Rochelle Avenue East

⑨

Bellagio

Vdara

Miracle
Mile

Tony n'
Tina's
Wedding

Lana Avenue

Harmon Avenue West

The Harmon

Planet
Hollywood

Harmon Avenue East

CityCenter

Veer Towers
& Crystals

Viva ELVIS
ARIA

Mandarin
Oriental

Signature at
MGM Grand

Monte Carlo

Rue de Monte Carlo

⑩

Il Fornaio
Panetteria

Showcase
Mall

GameWorks,
M&M's World

CSI: The Experience

New York-
New York

MGM Grand
Lion
Habitat

MGM
Grand

Wet Republic
Ultra Pool

TROPICANA

AVENUE

Excalibur

EXIT 37

Tropicana
The Mob
Experience

Reno Avenue West

Menopause:
The Musical

Reno

Avenue

East

King Tut's Tomb
and Museum

Luxor
Nurture,
The Spa
at Luxor

Pyramid
& Sphinx

Hacienda Avenue West

Fleur

Hacienda

Avenue

East

Shark
Reef

Mandalay
Bay

⑪

THEhotel

Spa Mandalay

Four
Seasons
Spa

Four Seasons Drive

Mandalay Bay
Convention
Center

EXIT
36

Dewey Drive East

"Welcome to Fabulous
Las Vegas" sign

McCarra
Internation
Airpo

Russell Road West

Bali Hai
Golf Club

⑫

0   500 m

0   500 yds

Ⓒ

Ⓓ

Ⓔ

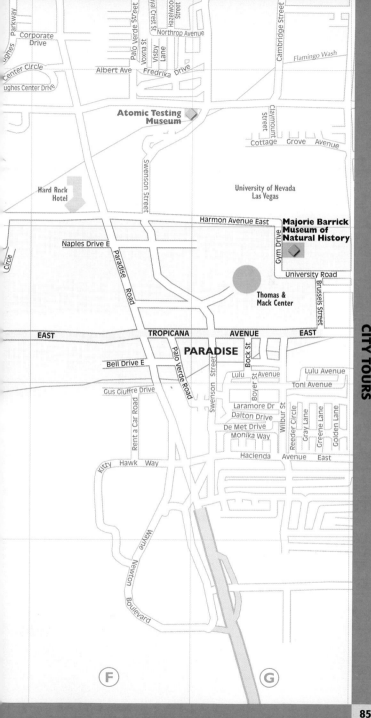

Corporate
Drive

Center Circle

ughes Center Drive

Albert Ave

Northrop Avenue

Fredrika Drive

Flamingo Wash

Cambridge Street

**Atomic Testing
Museum**

Claymount
Street

Cottage   Grove   Avenue

**Hard Rock
Hotel**

Swenson Street

University of Nevada
Las Vegas

Harmon Avenue East

**Majorie Barrick
Museum of
Natural History**

Naples Drive E

Gym Drive

University Road

Circle

Paradise   Road

Thomas &
Mack Center

Brussels Street

EAST   **TROPICANA**   **AVENUE**   **EAST**

PARADISE

Bock St

Bell Drive E

Palo Verde Road

Lulu   Avenue

Lulu Avenue

Swenson   Street

Boyer St

Toni Avenue

Gus Giuffre Drive

Rent a Car Road

Laramore Dr

Dalton Drive

De Met Drive

Monika Way

Wilbur St

Reeder Circle

Gray Lane

Greene Lane

Golden Lane

Hacienda   Avenue   East

Kitty   Hawk   Way

Wayne   Newton   Boulevard

(F)   (G)

SIGHTS AND EXPERIENCES

Excalibur (▷ 28)

Cross the drawbridge into this fantasyland to join King Arthur and his knights. Inside you will find costumed performers and one of the most popular dinner shows: the Tournament of Kings.

Lion Habitat (▷ 36)

See big cats up close in this lifelike habitat enclosed by a glass wall. Famous residents have included descendents of Metro, the lion that roared at the opening of every MGM film.

Luxor (▷ 38)

Ancient Egypt, the *Titanic* and the human body are all featured here. By night, a laser beam shoots from Luxor's apex and penetrates high into the sky; it's one of the most memorable sights of Vegas.

New York-New York (▷ 46)

The best of the Big Apple at one-third scale, and a sky-high roller coaster. You can loop the loop at high speed past the Statue of Liberty, the Empire State Building and the Brooklyn Bridge.

Shark Reef (▷ 54)

View sharks, rays and rainbow shoals of colorful tropical fish from inside the glass-walled Reef Tunnel at this exciting undersea world, with experts on hand to explain the mysteries of the deep.

Central Strip

Have a romantic and visually stunning day exploring the heart of The Strip, combining traditional Vegas razzmatazz with sophisticated modern art and architecture.

Morning
Begin your day at **Paris Las Vegas** (▷ 48–49). Have breakfast in **Mon Ami Gabi** (▷ 146), the only café with tables right on The Strip and great for people-watching over your *café au lait* and *croque-monsieur*. Ride the elevator up the Eiffel Tower for the best views all around the city and to the mountains beyond. Look for the thoughtfully placed lens-sized holes in the wire fence on each side of the observation platform, which allow you to take photos unobstructed.

Lunch
Take a Deuce bus up The Strip, past Bally's and Flamingo casinos, to **The Venetian** (▷ 58–59). Go on a gondola ride around the canals, browse the chic shopping arcades and have lunch at one of the cafés in St. Mark's Square, serenaded by performing street musicians. Live performances take place at regular intervals, with a timetable posted by the podium in the middle of the square.

Afternoon
Cross over the walkway to **The Mirage** (▷ 42–43), where you can see the rare animals in the **Dolphin Habitat and Secret Garden** (▷ 24–25) at the back of the resort. The dolphins are liveliest during feeding and show times, which take place regularly throughout the day, and if you're lucky you might see one of the keepers playing with the lion and tiger cubs in their enclosure.

Mid-afternoon

Turn right out of The Mirage and walk through **Caesars Palace** (▷ 18–19), with its Romanesque colonnades, talking statues and stylish boutiques. If it's a hot day, cool off in the magnificent Garden of the Gods pool area: six open-air swimming pools in manicured gardens decorated with mosaics, marble tiles, rotundas, statues and exclusive cabanas.

Dinner

Turn right out of Caesars Palace and cross the elevated footbridge over Flamingo Road to **Bellagio** (▷ 16–17). Watch the fountain display—hourly after dusk—to the music of perhaps Sinatra or Elton John. Have a buffet dinner inside the hotel, reputedly one of the best in town.

Evening

After dinner jump on the Deuce bus and go further down The Strip to **The Cosmopolitan** (▷ 154–155). Browse the sleek modern tower's super-chic lounges and shopping arcades by the main entrance. Sip a cocktail in one of its bars draped by the spectacular chandelier, which cascades down several stories in the hotel's atrium. Leaving The Cosmopolitan, walk right for a few minutes to the stunning **CityCenter** (▷ 22–23) and end the day in the **ARIA hotel** (▷ 153), watching **Viva ELVIS** (▷ 74), the latest show by the Cirque du Soleil, a tribute to the undisputed King of Las Vegas.

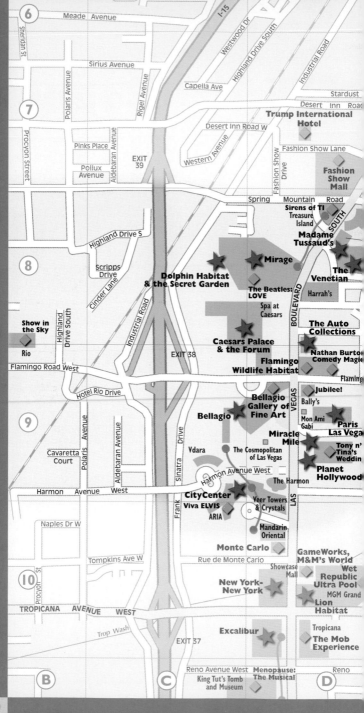

6 Meade Avenue

I-15

Westwood Dr

Highland Drive South

Sirius Avenue

Capella Ave

Industrial Road

Stardust

7 Polaris Avenue

Rigel Avenue

Desert Inn Road

Trump International Hotel

Desert Inn Road W

Western Avenue

Fashion Show Lane

Procyon Street

Pinks Place

Aldebaran Avenue

EXIT 39

Fashion Show Drive

Fashion Show Mall

Pollux Avenue

Spring Mountain Road

Sirens of TI Treasure Island

Madame Tussaud's

SOUTH

Highland Drive S

Mirage

Dolphin Habitat & the Secret Garden

The Beatles: LOVE

The Venetian

8 Scripps Drive

Cinder Lane

Spa at Caesars

Harrah's

BOULEVARD

Show in the Sky

Rio

Highland Drive South

Industrial Road

Caesars Palace & the Forum

The Auto Collections

Nathan Burton Comedy Magic

EXIT 38

Flamingo Wildlife Habitat

Flamingo

Flamingo Road West

Hotel Rio Drive

Bellagio Gallery of Fine Art

VEGAS

Jubilee!

Bally's

9 Polaris Avenue

Aldebaran Avenue

Bellagio

Mon Ami Gabi

Paris Las Vegas

Cavaretta Court

Sinatra Drive

Miracle Mile

Tony n' Tina's Wedding

Vdara

The Cosmopolitan of Las Vegas

Planet Hollywood

Harmon Avenue West

The Harmon

Harmon Avenue West

CityCenter

Veer Towers & Crystals

LAS

Naples Dr W

Frank Sinatra Drive

Viva ELVIS

ARIA

Mandarin Oriental

Monte Carlo

GameWorks, M&M's World

Tompkins Ave W

Rue de Monte Carlo

Showcase Mall

Wet Republic Ultra Pool

10 Procyon St

New York-New York

MGM Grand

Lion Habitat

TROPICANA AVENUE WEST

Trop Wash

Excalibur

Tropicana

The Mob Experience

EXIT 37

Reno Avenue West

King Tut's Tomb and Museum

Menopause: The Musical

Reno

B   C   D

90

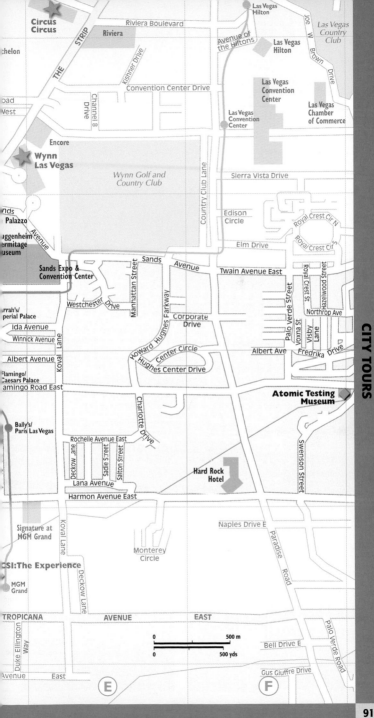

Central Strip Quick Reference Guide

The Auto Collections (▷ 14)
The world's largest and finest classic car showroom is housed inside the Imperial Palace. The collection includes automobiles of the rich and the famous.

Bellagio (▷ 16)
This Tuscan-themed resort takes you to the Italian town on Lake Como. Its highlight is the fountain display, with soaring jets beautifully choreographed to music.

Caesars Palace (▷ 18)
Fountains and Corinthian columns celebrate the glory of Rome. This sumptuous resort is packed with fine restaurants, shopping galleries, a spa and entertainment options.

CityCenter (▷ 22)
CityCenter is a gleaming architecturally designed complex of luxury hotels, entertainment and retail center, with world-class works of fine art.

Dolphin Habitat and the Secret Garden (▷ 24)
This is a comfortable, secure haven for big cats and dolphins. You can get close to the big cats, and the dolphins perform daily.

Madame Tussaud's (▷ 40)
Wax figures of the world's famous come to life in amusing scenes. Popular characters include stars who made it big in Vegas, such as Tom Jones and the Rat Pack.

The Mirage (▷ 42)
View exotic animals such as lions and tigers in a tropical atmosphere, and marvel at the simulated volcanic eruption in this Pacific island paradise.

Paris Las Vegas (▷ 48)
The stunningly accurate half-size model of the Eiffel Tower offers one of the best views over The Strip. Inside you can experience all the romance of Paris.

Planet Hollywood and Miracle Mile (▷ 50)
All the glamour of Hollywood is on show in Planet Hollywood, while Miracle Mile offers a relaxed and stylish shopping experience.

The Venetian (▷ 58)
Ride authentic gondolas around the canals in this re-creation of the Italian city. Marbled floors and Renaissance-style artworks adorn the lobbies and shopping arcades.

North Strip

Have an action-packed day of adrenaline thrills, art and culture in this long stretch of The Strip. Combine walking with hopping on and off the Deuce double-decker bus, using its 24-hour pass ($7).

Morning

Start your day at **The Arts Factory** (▷ 66), which has the latest in the city's alternative contemporary arts scene. Ask to see the huge tapestry of nighttime Vegas, by local artist Sola, which took her 8,000 hours to make, using wool from unraveled sweaters bought in charity shops. Walk left a couple of blocks along Charleston Boulevard to The Strip and hop on the Deuce bus, passing some of Vegas's famous **Wedding Chapels** (▷ 60–61), including **Viva Las Vegas** and the **Little White Wedding Chapel**.

Mid-morning

Get off the bus at the **Stratosphere Tower** (▷ 56–57). Ride the elevator up and go on the thrill rides, at more than 900ft (300m) above the ground. Its latest daredevil challenge is the Sky Jump: the highest controlled free fall in the world, leaping off the edge of the tower attached to a wire. For those with more sedate tastes, you can simply soak up the highest view in the city from the Observation Deck. Turn right out of the Stratosphere Tower and walk 10 to 15 minutes down The Strip. Along the way, drop in at **Bonanza Gifts** (▷ 117–118), which claims to be the biggest souvenir shop in the world. Over the road, look for the **Chapel of the Bells** (▷ 61), one of the most popular celebrity wedding chapels.

Lunch

Jump on a Deuce bus to **Circus Circus** (▷ 20–21). Ride the roller coasters in its Adventuredome, or take the plunge with a bungee jump from its high tower. Have lunch at one of its many snack eateries, or if you've worked up an appetite, gorge yourself at its buffet—one of the biggest in town—or on a meat feast at **The Steak House** (▷ 148).

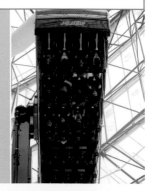

Afternoon

Turn right out of Circus Circus and walk 10 minutes down The Strip. Look for the tower of the **Trump International Hotel** (▷ 73–74) to your right and, opposite, the bronze arc of **Wynn Las Vegas** (▷ 62–63), the most luxurious hotel in the city. See its free water show—the Lake of Dreams—then explore its marbled halls, perhaps indulging in a cocktail at the magical **Parasol Up/ Parasol Down Bar**.

Late afternoon

Returning over The Strip, drop into the huge **Fashion Show Mall** (▷ 67), for a little bit of window-shopping in its glitzy boutiques and department stores, which include **Macy's** (▷ 120).

Evening

Have dinner at one of the Mall's many restaurants, such as the fun and lively diner **Johnny Rocket's** (▷ 145). Back on The Strip, cross over the elevated walkway again and walk a few minutes north to Wynn Las Vegas to round off your evening at the **Tryst** nightclub (▷ 135), favored hotspot of the city's well-heeled.

③

Shetland Road
Pinto Lane
RANCHO DRIVE SOUTH
Rancho Lane
Drive South
Rose St
Kenyon Place
Pinto Lane

Palomino Lane
Shetland Road
Tonopah
Valerie Street
Goldring Avenue
Willow Street
Alturas Avenue
Bearden Drive
Desert Lane

Trotter Circle

④ CHARLESTON BOULEVARD WEST

Cahlan Drive
Strong Drive
Edgewood Avenue
Park Circle
Shadow Lane
Ellis Avenue
Martin Luther King Boulevard South
Wall Street

Mason Avenue
Burton Avenue
Bryant Avenue
Colanthe Avenue
Gilmary Avenue
Waldman Avenue
Bannie Avenue
Pine St
Birch St
Silver Avenue
Westwood Drive
Western Avenue
Wyoming Aven

Oakey Boulevard West

Laurie Drive
Karli Drive

La Solana Way
Bryn Mawr Ave
Birch St
Ivanhoe Way
Kittle Way
Loch Lomond Way
Ne
Chica
Saint Lo
Boston Avenue V
Baltim

Bayo Ct
Mora Lane
Zafra Court
⑤ Fulano Way
Westund Drive
Kirkland Ave
Highland Avenue S
Clevela
Cincinnati A

Sidonia Avenue
De Osma Street
Lourdes Avenue
Glen Heather Way

Paseo del Prado

EXIT 40

SAHARA AVENUE WEST
Sahara Annex St
Alcoa Avenue
Teddy Drive
Palace Station
Westwood Drive
Western Ave
Drive

Kings Way
⑥
I-15
Rancho Drive South
Presidio Ave

Jamestown Way
Milo Way

Circus Circus Drive

Wyandote street

Circus Circus
Rivie
Riviera

THE STRIP

Echelon
Kishg
Conventi

Capella Ave
Highland Drive South
Industrial Road
Channel 8 Drive

Stardust Road
Desert Inn Road West
⑦
Desert Inn Road W

Trump International Hotel

Encore

Western Avenue
Fashion Show Drive
Fashion Show Lane
Wynn Las Vegas

EXIT 39
Fashion Show Mall
Johnny Rocket's ☐
LAS VEGAS BOULEVARD SOUTH
Wynn Golf and Country Club

Ⓒ Spring Mountain Road Ⓓ Sands Avenue Ⓔ
Treasure Island
Sirens of TI

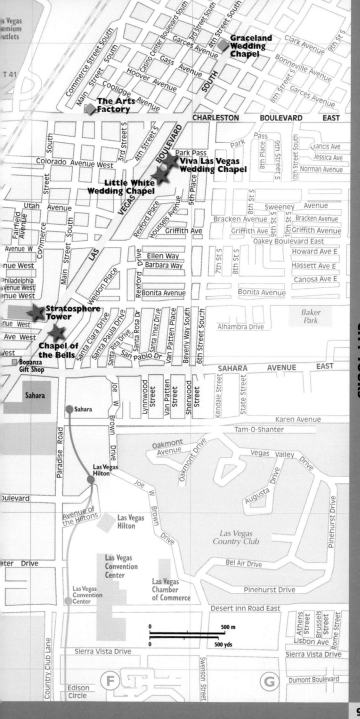

SIGHTS AND EXPERIENCES

CITY TOURS

Circus Circus (▷ 20)

Step inside the Big Top to find aerialists, acrobats, jugglers and clowns. Circus Circus is one of the most family-friendly resorts, with a high-speed roller coaster and other white-knuckle thrills in the Adventuredome, now also including a bungee jump tower.

Stratosphere Tower (▷ 56)

For extra excitement there are high-adrenaline rides at the top of the tallest free-standing observation tower in the US. From the platform looming more than 800ft (240m) over The Strip, you can challenge your nerves on four different rides, including Sky Jump—the highest controlled free fall in the world.

Wedding Chapels (▷ 60)

Getting married in a Las Vegas wedding chapel is an event you will never forget. From driving into a chapel in a pink Cadillac with Elvis at the wheel to getting hitched in Death Canyon, anything goes. You can even hire fancy dress costumes of your favorite movie characters to make it the ultimate fantasy experience.

Wynn Las Vegas (▷ 62)

This luxury resort brims with opulence. It's not just one of the tallest buildings in the city, it also has its own 18-hole golf course, a lagoon backed by a man-made mountain and even a superb collection of original masterpieces on the premises.

CITY TOURS

Downtown

Discover the city's roots at a new museum dedicated to its shady Mob associations, and a collection of its original neon signs. End your day here after dusk, as a blaze of neon and pounding music fills the Fremont Street arched roof.

Morning
Start at El Cortez, the only Downtown property whose exterior has remained mostly unaltered. Have breakfast at **The Beat** (▷ 140), on the opposite corner of Fremont Street and Las Vegas Boulevard South. Browse its retro posters and secondhand LPs for sale, and check out the modern artwork in the adjoining Emergency Arts Gallery. Leaving The Beat, turn left up Las Vegas Boulevard and first left again on Stewart Avenue, with the City Hall on the corner.

Mid-morning
Cross over and on the next block is the old Post Office/Federal Building—a neoclassical structure built in 1933. Visit **The Mob Museum** (▷ 44–45). This major new collection charts the rise and fall of organized crime in Las Vegas, located in the former courthouse where an historic hearing marked the beginning of the end of the Mob gangster era.

Lunch
Continue to the end of Stewart Avenue and at the T-junction with Main Street is **Main Street Station** (▷ 157). This is one of the most floridly decorated hotels in Downtown; stained-glass windows and chandeliers add color and sparkle to its casino, and its magnificent bar has a bronze sculpted wild boar as its centerpiece. Have lunch at one of the restaurants, then pick up a map at the front desk and take a self-guided tour of the antiques collection.

Afternoon
Continue along Main Street. On the right is an antique railcar, with one private carriage used by Buffalo Bill Cody and Annie Oakley. Next on the right you come to the Plaza hotel, where the Union Pacific Railroad Depot stood, once the focal point of Downtown. Cross the road to the Golden Gate, one of the oldest remaining hotels in the area.

Mid-afternoon

Turn down Fremont Street under the huge canopy. Look for the neon signs, including **Vegas Vic and Vegas Vicki** (▷ **Neon Boneyard Park**, 71–72). Further down is the **Golden Nugget** (▷ 68), Binion's and the Fremont, three of Downtown's most nostalgic hotel casinos. You'll see people whizzing overhead on the **Flightlinez** zip line (▷ 67–68), the Street's latest white-knuckle attraction.

Evening

Stay for the light-and-sound show of the **Fremont Street Experience** (▷ 30–31), which fills the canopy in a blaze of color, (6pm and then hourly till midnight). Have dinner, either at **Binion's Café** (▷ 141), an economical option inside Binion's, or splash out at **Hugo's Cellar** (▷ 144), in the Four Queens Hotel, opposite. Proceed to the end. At the intersection with Las Vegas Boulevard are more neon signs, such as Aladdin's Lamp and the Hacienda Horse and Rider.

Martin Luther King Boulevard North

Wezer Drive

Freeman Avenue
Leonard Avenue
D Street

Owens Avenue West

Harrison Avenue

Gold Avenue

Van Buren Ave W
Jackson Avenue

Van Buren Avenue West
Jackson Avenue

C Street

B Street

Monroe Ave W
Madison Avenue

Monroe Avenue W

Madison Ave

F Street
E Street
D Street

A Street

Jefferson Avenue
Adams Avenue West

Jefferson Avenue

Cunningham Drive

J St
I Street
H Street

Washington Avenue West

M St
3S N

Reed Pl
1st St

Morgan Avenue West
Gerson Ave
Mc Williams Avenue West

Morgan Avenue

EXIT 44

EXIT 43

Wilson Ave

Main Street North

(1)

I-15

(2)

Bonanza Road West

EXIT 76C

Mesquite Avenue West

EXIT 76B

EXIT 42

ORAN

**MAIN STREET
STATION**

F St

K

1st Street N

DOWNTOWN

Ogden West

Plaza Hotel

Casino Center Boulevard N

The Mol
Museum

Martin Luther King Boulevard South

Grand Central Parkway South

Greyhound
Bus Terminal

Golden
Gate

Binion's
Cafe

Hugo's
Cellar

Flightline

Golden Nugget

Casino

Neonopo

**Fremont Street
Experience**

Carson

Neon
Museum Av

(3)

Bonneville Avenue West

Main Street South

1st Street South

Lewis Ave

3rd Street South
4th Street South

6th Street South

7th S

Cla

Las Vegas
Premium
Outlets

Carces Avenue

Gass Avenue

**Graceland
Wedding
Chapel**

Bonnev

8th Street S
Gar

EXIT 41

Commerce Street South

Main Street South

Hoover Avenue

Coolidge Avenue

**The Arts
Factory**

3rd Street S

4th Street S

BOULEVARD

CHARLESTO

(4)

Wall Street

Colorado Avenue West

Park Pass

Park

Pass

8th Place

9th Place

10th Street South

Western Avenue

3rd Street South

4th Street S

VEGAS

Park Pass
**Viva Las Vegas
Wedding Chapel**

5th Place

**Little White
Wedding Chapel**

Rexford Place

Houssels Avenue

Griffith Ave

8th St S
9th St S

10th St S

Sweeney

Bracken Avenue

Griffith Ave

7th St S
8th St S

Oakey Boulevar

(5)

Wyoming Ave West

Fairfield Avenue

Utah Avenue

Commerce Street

Main Street

New York
Avenue West

LAS

Ellen Way

Barbara Way

7th St S
8th St S

(E)

Chicago Avenue West

(F)

(G)

Reynolds Avenue

Webb Avenue

East

Owens Avenue East

Foremaster Lane

Lions Memorial Park

Gragson Avenue

Searles Avenue East

Demetrius Avenue East
Theresa Ave E
Jansen Avenue East
Brady Avenue
Brady Ave E

Washington Avenue E

Old Mormon Fort

Las Vegas Natural History Museum

Lied Discovery Children's Museum

Cashman Field Center Stadium

Harris Avenue

Neon Boneyard Park

Harris Avenue

Mc Williams Avenue E

Wilson Ave E

Neon Museum
La Concha
Visitor Center

EXIT 75

Wilson Ave E

Ryan Avenue

Bonanza Road East

Linden Avenue East

Walnut Avenue

EXPRESSWAY

Cedar Avenue

Poplar Avenue East

Elm Avenue

Mesquite Avenue E

The Beat

El Cortez

Marlin Avenue

Stewart Ave

Ash Ave

Ogden Ave E

Berkley Ave

Isabelle Ave

Sunrise Ave

Ogden Avenue East

Fremont Street

Carson Avenue

ridger Avenue

Lewis Avenue

Carson Avenue

Lewis Ave

Sunrise Avenue

Fremont Street

Maryland Parkway

Rue 13 S

Lewis Ave

BOULEVARD

EAST

Ballard Drive

ncis Avenue Francis Avenue

Peyton Drive

ssica Ave Jessica Ave

Houston Drive

orman Ave Norman Avenue

Franklin Avenue

Franklin Avenue

Wengert Ave

Wengert Avenue

Sweeney Avenue

Sweeney Ave

Bracken Ave

Bracken Avenue

cken Ave

Griffith Ave

Griffith Avenue

ffith Ave

ward Ave Howard Ave

Hassett Ave

Canosa Ave

(H)

(J)

Bonita Ave

Downtown Quick Reference Guide

Downtown (▷ 26)
If you're looking for classic Las Vegas, this is the place to find it. Iconic neon signs form a self-guided tour of the historic neighborhood, and you can explore some of the original casinos. The ongoing regeneration program will include a world-class performing arts center.

Fremont Street Experience (▷ 30)
Be dazzled by this amazing light-and-sound show. Daily at dusk the arched roof of Fremont Street bursts into life with two million lights flashing and animating to the pulse of music. You can watch the free hourly show as you browse the stores, cafés and casinos.

Las Vegas Natural History Museum (▷ 34)
Five animated dinosaurs take center stage here, including a T-Rex. In addition to all the stuffed animals exhibited in this excellent museum, there is a live animal petting area and a Marine Life Gallery, featuring leopard sharks and a shark egg hatchery.

The Mob Museum (▷ 44)
Meet the gangsters and the law enforcement officials who finally broke the criminals' control of old Vegas. This groundbreaking new museum is based in the original courthouse where the historic hearings revealing the stunning scale and power of organized crime gripped the nation in 1950.

CITY TOURS

The Golden Nugget was the first luxury hotel in Las Vegas

Further Afield

On this scenic day's drive out of Las Vegas you can witness the man-made wonder of the Hoover Dam, explore Lake Mead, then relax at an Italianesque spa village overlooking Lake Las Vegas. TIP: Arrive at Hoover Dam by 9am, as long queues for the Dam Tour form later in the morning (you can't buy tickets online, although other tours, such as the Power Plant Tour, can be purchased on the official website: www.usbr.gov/lc/hooverdam).

Morning
Drive out of the city southeastward on US93 for 30 miles (48km) to **Hoover Dam** (▷ 32–33). From the city center go along East Flamingo Road toward Audrie Street, picking up the I-515, which merges with US93, via Henderson. Continue on US93 for 20 miles (32km) to Boulder City, turning left at the second set of traffic lights for another 5 miles (8km) to the turning (just past Hacienda Hotel) onto Nevada State Route 172— the Hoover Dam Access Road.

Lunch
Continue on NV SR172 for 2 miles (3km) to the Dam. Park in the car park ($7 charge) opposite the Visitor Center, and take the guided tour of Hoover Dam. Have lunch afterward at the snack bar next to the parking lot.

Afternoon
Leaving Hoover Dam, return along the same road toward Boulder City, turning right after a few miles onto Lake Mead Drive (SR 564), the scenic lakeshore road that runs along the west side of Lake Mead, part of the **Lake Mead National Recreation Area** (▷ 33). Drop in at the Alan Bible Visitor Center, just past the junction, to pick up information about visiting Lake Mead. Drive along the lakeshore and stop along the way at designated parking spots, from where you can walk on lakeside paths or take a boat excursion. Continue around the lake and take the second right-hand turn a few miles after leaving the Entrance Station, signposted to Lake Las Vegas Parkway.

Mid-afternoon
Follow this short road to the **Ravella**, an Italian-style spa resort, with its picturesque tile-roofed villas and towers, upscale arts and craft shops, restaurants and marina.

Dinner
Dine at the hotel restaurant or one of the seven informal eateries clustered around the cobbled pathways.

Evening
Return to Las Vegas, turning right onto Lake Mead Drive, which joins US93 after about 9 miles (15km), turning right toward the city. Continue for another 9 miles (15km) to the junction with Flamingo Road, which leads back to Las Vegas Boulevard. Alternatively, stay the night at the Ravella Resort, to enjoy the lakeside tranquility and unwind in the spa and swimming pool, after your busy day.

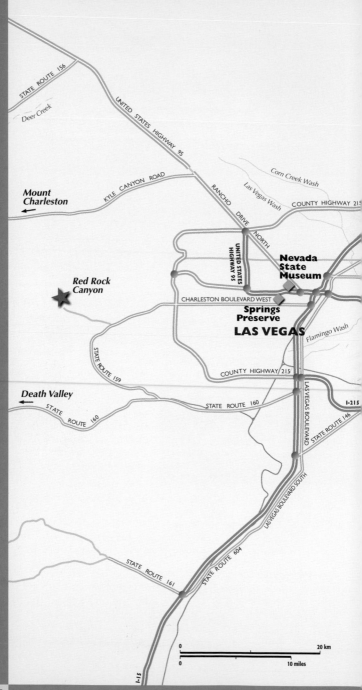

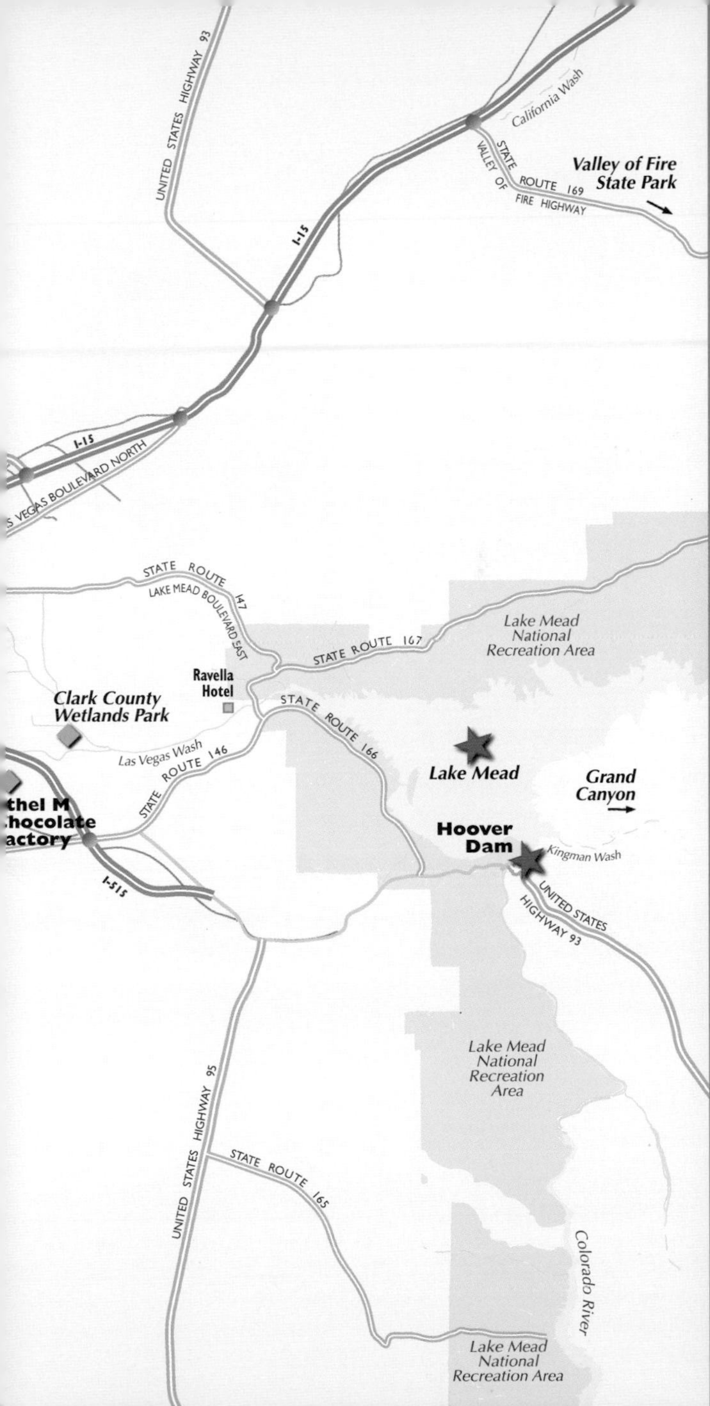

United States Highway 93

California Wash

State Route 169

Valley of Fire Highway

Valley of Fire State Park →

I-15

I-15

Las Vegas Boulevard North

State Route 147

Lake Mead Boulevard East

State Route 167

Lake Mead National Recreation Area

Ravella Hotel

State Route 166

Clark County Wetlands Park

State Route 146

Las Vegas Wash

★ **Lake Mead**

Grand Canyon →

thel M hocolate actory

I-515

Hoover Dam ★

Kingman Wash

United States Highway 93

United States Highway 95

State Route 165

Lake Mead National Recreation Area

Colorado River

Lake Mead National Recreation Area

Further Afield Quick Reference Guide

SIGHTS AND EXPERIENCES

Hoover Dam and Lake Mead
(▷ 32)

This is a must-see getaway from the neon lights. Less than an hour from the city, the Hoover Dam is one of the world's engineering wonders, and the powerhouse keeping Las Vegas going 24 hours a day. Adjacent Lake Mead, created by the damming of the Colorado River, offers a range of boating, fishing and water-sports activities.

Red Rock Canyon (▷ 52)

You'll find these spectacular rock formations only a 20-minute drive from Vegas. The striking layers of red sandstone and gray-green limestone were formed 65 million years ago, contrasting with the spiky desert plantlife, including yucca and Joshua trees. Today, the canyon is protected as a National Conservation Area, offering great outdoor activities, including hiking, rock climbing and biking.

MORE TO SEE	64

Clark County Wetlands Park
Ethel M. Chocolate Factory
Nevada State Museum
Springs Preserve

SHOP	112

Jewelry
Jana's Jade Gallery
Shopping Malls
Boulevard Mall
Las Vegas Chinatown Plaza

Meadows Mall
Town Square
Souvenirs
Harley-Davidson

Entertainment and Sports
Orleans Arena
Golf
Angel Park Golf Club

Las Vegas National
Royal Links Golf Club

The dazzling blue waters of Lake Mead

Dior

Shop

Whether you're looking for the best local products, a department store or a quirky boutique, you'll find them all in Las Vegas. In this section shops are listed alphabetically.

Introduction

Retail therapy in Vegas has soared in recent years, with an influx of designer stores and hundreds of well-known retailers and flagship department stores that have put the city firmly on the shopping map. Shopping in Vegas mainly revolves around treading the elegant walkways of the numerous malls. As for choice, it depends more on how much money you have to spend and how far you are prepared to travel than on what you are looking to buy.

A Unique Experience

Most of The Strip hotels have their own shopping opportunities, some more spectacular than others. There is simply no other city in the world where you are able to shop under an artificial sky among Roman architecture and talking statues, or journey between shops by gondola, all within a short distance of each other. Hotel malls in Vegas offer more than just great stores: all sorts of entertainment is lined up to amuse you as you shop, but this is reflected in the cost of the goods. There are other malls on The Strip not attached to any particular hotel, such as the huge Fashion Show Mall (▷ 67).

Let's Get Serious

Serious shoppers should venture a few blocks away from The Strip, where they will discover

PAWNSHOPS

The nature of Vegas means it attracts lots of pawnshops. Many are opposite gambling areas—open 24 hours—waiting to unload desperate gamblers of their possessions for quick cash. Items that are not reclaimed within about 120 days are sold. You will discover all sorts of bizarre items at pawnshops, but jewelry, musical instruments and electrical equipment are the most common. Gone are the days of acquiring these items at rock-bottom prices, although you might pick up the odd bargain.

Clockwise from top: The Grand Canal Shoppes at The Venetian line a quarter-mile (400m) replica of the Grand Canal; luxury shopping at Dior on Via Bellagio;

more vast malls that are less crowded and filled with major retailers and specialist stores selling practical items at more realistic prices. Clothes range from daring and trendy to boutique exclusives, and the very latest in shoes, lingerie, jewelry and designer glasses complete a look suitable to hit the Vegas scene. True bargainhunters should head for one of the factory outlets (▷ 120), where top designer clothes, among other things, can be bought at 25–75 percent off. Items for the home, electronics and footwear are particularly good value. A lot of the merchandise is end of line or last season's items. Make sure you are getting top quality and not seconds or damaged goods. Some outlet malls have a shuttle service from hotels on The Strip.

Souvenirs and Gifts

At the other end of the scale from the classy boutiques are the endless souvenir shops along Las Vegas Boulevard, each selling the same mass-produced card decks and key rings. Every hotel also has a gift shop, with logo merchandise that exploits themes to the extreme, while casino gift shops are generally more elegant and expensive.

SHOP

THAT SPECIAL GIFT

Although Vegas is not known for one particular souvenir—apart from the kitsch in its gift shops—given the time and money, you can buy almost anything here. Gambling merchandise abounds in every guise and quality leather jackets bearing logos are popular. Wine makes a safe gift as Vegas has the largest public collection of fine wines in the world. You might discover that unique collectible you've always wanted—a signed Michael Jordan basketball or autographed Beatles poster. Precious jewels for sale in the city have included Ginger Rogers' engagement ring and the Moghul Emerald (the world's largest carved emerald), but these would break the bank—unless you strike it lucky, of course.

the mosaic-tiled floor on Via Bellagio; get great discounts at Las Vegas Premium Outlets; Gucci on Via Bellagio; La Scarpa shoe shop on Via Bellagio

Directory

SHOP

Shopping A-Z

99 CENT ONLY STORE
www.99only.com
Las Vegas isn't all designer shops and expensive boutiques. Take a look at this huge store where literally everything is just 99 cents. With a boom in sales at branches across the country, the store stocks groceries, beauty products, gifts and household supplies.
➕ Off map at J4 ✉ 45 North Nellis Boulevard, off East Charleston Boulevard ☎ 702/459-1599 🚌 206

ABERCROMBIE & FITCH
www.abercrombie.com
The range of clothing for young aspiring men and women features the company's preppy-style look in hoodies, sweats, shirts and jeans.
➕ D7 ✉ Fashion Show Mall, 3200 Las Vegas Boulevard South ☎ 702/650-6509 🚌 Deuce

ALPACA IMPORTS
www.alpacapetes.com
You'll find quality handcrafted alpaca yarn products from all over the world here. Rugs are the signature product, but there are also slippers, sweaters and soft furnishings.
➕ D9 ✉ Miracle Mile, 3663 Las Vegas Boulevard South ☎ 702/862-8297 🚌 Deuce

THE ATTIC
www.atticvintage.com
There is a hidden treasure in just about every corner in this fascinating place, including a good range of retro and vintage clothing, interesting collectibles, furniture, jewelry, old radios, TVs, cameras and electrical appliances.
➕ F3 ✉ 1025 South Main Street ☎ 702/388-4088 🚌 108

BARNES & NOBLE
This is one of several Vegas branches of the colossally well-stocked general bookstore. It has impressive children's and best-seller sections.
➕ G7 ✉ 3860 South Maryland Parkway ☎ 702/734-2900 🚌 109

BEBE
Sleek designs and curve-hugging wear inspired by the latest trends feature at this sassy boutique.
➕ D7 ✉ Fashion Show Mall, 3200 Las Vegas Boulevard South ☎ 702/892-8083 🚌 Deuce

BETSEY JOHNSON
Flowing fabrics with beaded and embroidered detail are very much the style at this wacky shop for a wacky clientele.
➕ D7 ✉ Fashion Show Mall, 3200 Las Vegas Boulevard South ☎ 702/735-3338 🚌 Deuce

BONANZA GIFTS
www.worldslargestgiftshop.com
The self-styled "largest souvenir store in the world" has a mind-boggling array of tacky mementos.

HOTEL SHOPPING

You will find many familiar stores in hotel malls, such as Gap, Victoria's Secret, Tommy Bahama and Levi's Original, and the classier places will have designer boutiques like Prada and Hermès, too. You won't find the big department stores here, but you'll be able to buy a good range of items, including more mundane requirements such as toiletries, cosmetics and magazines. Souvenirs may include pieces that reflect the hotel's theme, or merchandise from the permanent shows and visiting entertainers.

The Forum Shops in Caesars Palace, of which Carolina Herrera is one

It's worth a visit just to see how tasteless it can all get.

⊞ E6 ⊠ 2440 Las Vegas Boulevard South ☎ 702/385-7359 🚌 Deuce

BOULEVARD MALL

www.boulevardmall.com

The oldest mall in Las Vegas is popular with customers in the southeast of the city for its moderate price tags. It has around 140 shops, including department stores JC Penney, Macy's, Marshall's and Sears.

⊞ H8 ⊠ 3528 Maryland Parkway ☎ 702/735-7430 🚌 109

CAROLINA HERRERA

This store is dedicated to Herrera's lifestyle collection for men and women. The range includes chic tailored suits, glam evening wear, cotton shirts and accessories.

⊞ C8–D8 ⊠ The Forum Shops, 3570 Las Vegas Boulevard South ☎ 702/894-5242 🚌 Deuce

CASTLE WALK

Well and truly carrying on the medieval theme, this mall includes a range of gift shops selling magic tricks and accoutrements, medieval replica swords and shields (and the occasional suit of armor).

⊞ D10 ⊠ Excalibur, 3850 Las Vegas Boulevard South ☎ 702/597-7850 🚌 Deuce

CHIHULY STORE

This shop has a good representation of the respected glass sculptor's vibrant hand-blown pieces. It is fitting that Chihuly opened his first gallery here—his biggest sculpture hangs from the Bellagio's lobby ceiling (▷ 16–17).

⊞ C9–D9 ⊠ Via Fiore, Bellagio, 3600 Las Vegas Boulevard South ☎ 702/693-7995 🚌 Deuce

FIELD OF DREAMS

This is the place for one-off sport and celebrity memorabilia, such as an electric guitar signed by musician Carlos Santana or a jersey autographed by football player Dan Marino.

⊞ B8 ⊠ Masquerade Village, Rio, 3700 West Flamingo Road ☎ 702/777-7777 🚌 202

THE FUNK HOUSE

www.thefunkhouselasvegas.com

One of the best antiques stores in the city is the creation of Cindy Funkhouser. Her growing collection includes some interesting items from the late-1950s and early-

1960s, including furniture, glass, jewelry, rugs, paintings and toys. Enjoy browsing.
✚ F4 ✉ 1228 South Casino Center Boulevard ☎ 702/678-6278 🚌 105, 108, 116

GAMBLER'S GENERAL STORE
www.gamblersgeneralstore.com
What better souvenir of your trip to Las Vegas than something with a gambling theme? Take home a roulette wheel, blackjack table, poker chip tray or slot machine. The used-card decks and gambling chips from major casinos are good, inexpensive buys.
✚ F3 ✉ 800 South Main Street ☎ 702/382-9903 🚌 108

GIANNI VERSACE
The late designer's Italian style is obvious in the garments sold here, all made from the finest fabrics. The company's signature lion's head appears on everything.
✚ C8–D8 ✉ The Forum Shops, 3570 Las Vegas Boulevard South ☎ 702/932-5757 🚌 Deuce

GRAND CANAL SHOPPES
This chic Italian-theme mall stretches along a replica of Venice's Grand Canal. Here you'll find over 80 of the most exclusive stores in the world, ranging from Davidoff cigars to designer shoes.

✚ D8 ✉ The Venetian, 3355 Las Vegas Boulevard South ☎ 702/414-1000 🚌 Deuce

LE GRAND JEWELS
Le Grand Jewels is an upscale jewelry store specializing in top-quality pearls, diamonds and gold items, and offering personalized sizing and fitting.
✚ D9 ✉ Bally's, 3645 Las Vegas Boulevard South ☎ 702/736-7355 🚌 Deuce

HARLEY-DAVIDSON
www.lvhd.com
The world's largest Harley store has a vast array of merchandise and bikes on display. You can even rent a bike here if you can't afford to buy.
✚ J6 ✉ 2605 South Eastern Avenue ☎ 702/431-8500 🚌 110

HOUDINI MAGIC
Every 15 minutes until midnight you can watch live magic shows, and then buy your own magic tricks from the selection of sleight-of-hand tricks available for sale.
✚ D10 ✉ MGM Grand, Starlane Mall, 3799 Las Vegas Boulevard South ☎ 702/891-7777 🚌 Deuce

JANA'S JADE GALLERY
This gallery sells an unusual and fascinating selection of hand-crafted jade jewelry.

Come to Mandalay Place for upscale shopping and dining

🚩 A8–B8 ✉ Las Vegas Chinatown Plaza, 4255 Spring Mountain Road ☎ 702/227-9198 🚌 203

LAS VEGAS CHINATOWN PLAZA

www.lvchinatown.com
This cluster of more than 20 Asian restaurants, shops and food stores is located just a few blocks west of Central Strip. You can pick up jade jewelry, clothes, ornaments, Chinese foods and herbs, and eat at one of the good-value restaurants specializing in cuisine from China, Japan, Korea, the Philippines and Vietnam.
🚩 A8–B8 ✉ 4255 Spring Mountain Road ☎ 702/221-8448 🚌 203

LAS VEGAS PREMIUM OUTLETS

www.premiumoutlets.com
Save 25 to 65 percent at this large designer and name-brand outlet, whose names include Ann Taylor, Dolce and Gabbana, Guess, Adidas and Elie Tahari.
🚩 E3 ✉ 875 South Grand Central Parkway ☎ 702/474-7500 🚌 108, 109 from DTC

M&M'S WORLD

www.mms.com
A tourist attraction as well as a candy store and chocolate lover's dream, this place has a huge selection of well-known confectionery brands, including a vast array of liqueur-filled chocolates and, of course, M&M's.
🚩 D10 ✉ Showcase Mall, 3785 Las Vegas Boulevard South ☎ 702/736-7611 🚌 Deuce

MACY'S

www.macys.com
The choice at this department store is extensive; all your fashion needs, for men, women and children are here, as well as accessories, shoes and homeware.
🚩 D7 ✉ Fashion Show Mall, 3200 Las Vegas Boulevard South ☎ 702/731-5111 🚌 Deuce

MAIN STREET ANTIQUES

www.mainstreetantiqueslv.com
This large store on two floors offers treasures from more than 40 dealers. Lots of Vegas collectibles can be found, plus

items from around the world. Check out the rare items from the 1950s and 1960s.

⊞ F3　✉ 500 South Main Street
☎ 702/382-1882　🚌 108

MANDALAY PLACE

A sky bridge connecting Mandalay Bay with the Luxor is home to a number of superior retailers. These include top designer names in men's and women's fashion, and renowned jewelry stores, as well as other specialties.

⊞ D11　✉ Mandalay Bay, 3950 Las Vegas Boulevard South　☎ 702/632-7800
🚌 Deuce

MANOLO BLAHNIK

Timeless and beautifully made, Manolo's sexy shoes are as famous as the women who wear them. The store is located inside the exclusive Wynn Esplanade.

⊞ D7–E7　✉ Wynn Las Vegas, 3131 Las Vegas Boulevard South　☎ 702/770-7000
🚌 Deuce

MASQUERADE VILLAGE

Stroll down the tiled streets here to find quirky places such as the Nawlins Store, carrying voodoo supplies and good-luck charms. Elsewhere in the mall, sportswear and memorabilia are on sale.

⊞ B8　✉ Rio, 3700 West Flamingo Road
☎ 702/777-7777　🚌 202

MEADOWS MALL

www.meadowsmall.com

This is yet another huge shopping mall made up of more than 140 main-street names and well-known department stores.

⊞ B2　✉ 4300 Meadows Lane (at intersection of Valley View and US95)
☎ 702/878-3331　🚌 103, 104, 402

MIKIMOTO

Exquisite Akoya cultured pearls and South Sea pearl jewelry are sold here among other gift items.

⊞ D8　✉ Grand Canal Shoppes, The Venetian, 3355 Las Vegas Boulevard South
☎ 702/414-3900　🚌 Deuce

OSCAR DE LA RENTA

This renowned designer, famous for his delicate and opulent collections of women's clothes and accessories, has chosen the Wynn Esplanade to display his exquisite finery.

⊞ D7–E7　✉ Wynn Las Vegas, 3131 Las Vegas Boulevard South　☎ 702/770-7000
🚌 Deuce

PEARL FACTORY

See how pearls are cultured before you make your decision, and have them mounted in the setting of your choice. Hawaiian heirloom jewelry is also displayed.

⊞ D10　✉ MGM Grand, Starlane Mall, 3799 Las Vegas Boulevard South
☎ 702/891-0344　🚌 Deuce

PEARL MOON BOUTIQUE

It's a bit on the pricey side, but the selection of swimwear, hats, sunglasses and sandals here is better quality than you'll find at other shops on The Strip.

ARTS AND CRAFTS

Las Vegas has plenty of places where you can buy fine artworks. Classical and contemporary art and sculpture are sold in many shopping malls, including the Fashion Show Mall, Forum Shops, Grand Canal Shoppes and other outlets on and off The Strip. The Arts Factory (▷ 66) has many galleries and studios and holds a special monthly late-opening evening.

CULTURAL CORRIDOR

On Las Vegas Boulevard between Bonanza Road and Washington Avenue is a hub of seven institutions that promote art and history in the city. The Cashman Center, an arts and sporting center; Las Vegas Library; Las Vegas Natural History Museum (▷ 34–35); Lied Discovery Children's Museum (▷ 69–70); Neon Boneyard Park (▷ 71–72); Old Mormon Fort (▷ 72); and the Reed Whipple Cultural Center, which encourages local, regional and national artists. For more information visit www.culturalcorridorvegas.org.

✚ D11 ✉ Mandalay Bay, 3950 Las Vegas Boulevard South ☎ 702/632-7777 🚌 Deuce

RAINBOW FEATHER DYEING COMPANY

www.rainbowfeatherco.com
Feathers of every hue and shade are made into boas, ornaments and jewelry, as well as flights for archery. Master feather-crafter Bill Girard creates wonderful accessories, which are worn by Las Vegas showgirls and Cirque du Soleil acrobats.
✚ F3 ✉ 1036 South Main Street ☎ 702/598-0988 🚌 108

REED KRAKOFF

www.simon.com/mall/landing/224
This familiar favorite sells women's luxury ready-to-wear fashion, as well as handbags, small leather goods, shoes, sunglasses, watches and jewelry.
✚ C8–D8 ✉ The Forum Shops, Caesars Palace, 3570 Las Vegas Boulevard South ☎ 702/644-4153 🚌 Deuce

SAM ASH

www.samashmusic.com
Sam Ash is a musicians' playground, stacked high with guitars, amps, drums and brass and wind instruments of every conceivable brand.
✚ H6 ✉ 2747 Maryland Parkway ☎ 702/734-0007 🚌 109

SERGE'S SHOWGIRL WIGS

www.showgirlwigs.com
Choose from around 10,000 wigs, in all shapes and shades and top it with a showgirl headdress.
✚ G6 ✉ Commercial Center Plaza, 953 East Sahara Avenue ☎ 702/732-1015 🚌 204

SHOPPES AT THE PALAZZO

www.theshoppesatthepalazzo.com
Stylish shopping awaits at the Palazzo, anchored by Barneys New York, as well as more than 60 international boutiques, including Christian Louboutin and Jimmy Choo.
✚ D8 ✉ The Palazzo, 3325 Las Vegas Boulevard South ☎ 702/414-4525 🚌 Deuce

SILVER HORSE ANTIQUES

Take a look at this fascinating store, with lamps, furniture, glass collectibles and other items hidden in a real treasure house.
✚ H4 ✉ 1651 East Charleston Boulevard ☎ 702/385-2700 🚌 206

STREET OF DREAMS

Street of Dreams is a modest mall with clothing boutiques, jewelry stores and a cake shop, plus an outlet of Harley-Davidson, the famous motorcycle manufacturer.
✚ D10 ✉ Monte Carlo, 3770 Las Vegas Boulevard South ☎ 702/730-7777 🚌 Deuce

SUGAR FACTORY

www.parislasvegas.com

Nestled at the foot of the Eiffel Tower, this new candy store is a sticky wonderland for anyone with a sweet tooth. As well as all its beautifully packaged chocolates and candies, it has a brasserie and the Chocolate Lounge, with luxury imported chocolate.

🔢 D9 ✉ Paris Las Vegas, 3655 Las Vegas Boulevard South ☎ 702/331-5100 🚌 Deuce

TEAVANA

www.teavana.com

This is tea heaven and a must for all aficionados of the brew. There are white, black and green varieties, plus organic, herbal and many more. The teapots, mugs and storage tins make ideal gifts.

🔢 D7 ✉ Fashion Show Mall, 3200 Las Vegas Boulevard South ☎ 702/369-9732 🚌 Deuce

TOWN SQUARE

www.townsquarelasvegas.com

Colonial and Spanish-style facades, enhanced by antique streetlights, conceal an eclectic mix of stores, restaurants and bars. A small central park houses a children's playground and picnic area. There is also a cinema on site.

🔢 D12 ✉ 6605 Las Vegas Boulevard South ☎ 702/269-5000 🍴 Numerous restaurants and cafés 🚌 104, Deuce

VIA BELLAGIO

This opulent mall has exquisite fashion and jewelry collections from world-renowned designers Chanel, Gucci, Prada, Tiffany & Co. and many more.

🔢 C9–D9 ✉ Bellagio, 3600 Las Vegas Boulevard South ☎ 702/693-7111 🚌 Deuce

WYNN ESPLANADE

An endless list of exclusive names can be found at this luxury hotel mall. Take your pick from the likes of Manolo Blahnik, Alexander McQueen, Cartier, Chanel and Louis Vuitton, or the Ferrari-Maserati dealership.

🔢 D7–E7 ✉ Wynn Las Vegas, 3131 Las Vegas Boulevard South ☎ 702/770-7000 🚌 Deuce

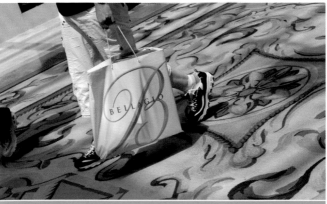

The Bellagio's luxury shopping mall, Via Bellagio

Tooters
Only

Monster Yard
$16.75
Refill $13.75
46 oz.

Pilsner Glass
$10.75
Refill $7.75
20 oz.

Giant Mug
$13.75
Refill $10.75
36 oz.

Entertainment

Once you've done with sightseeing for the day, you'll find lots of other great things to do with your time in this chapter, even if all you want to do is relax with a drink. In this section establishments are listed alphabetically.

ENTERTAINMENT

Introduction

Vegas really comes alive after the sun goes down, and some of the best attractions are to be found during the twilight hour. Soak up a pulsating nightlife scene like no other—this is a great place to party.

Endless Variety

From casino lounges to clubs, pubs and cocktail bars, the possibilities for a fun night out are endless. Numerous nightspots provide the chance to dance until dawn. Ultra lounges are the latest trend, stylish spaces that attract a cutting-edge crowd, where DJs spin their vinyl but conversation takes priority. But this is Sin City, and there are several, not very well-concealed, strip joints scattered throughout. These can, however, be disregarded amid the sheer scale of everything else.

Only the Best

Las Vegas is infamous for its stage extravaganzas, which incorporate unbelievable special effects and have attracted some of the world's hottest superstars. Shows vary from Broadway musicals and spectacular productions to comedy and magic. Vegas also plays host to some of the world's biggest special events, such as world championship boxing matches. The top shows can be expensive and the most popular often need to be reserved well in advance. But the best

GAMING

Where else could you continually be refueled with free drinks as you play the blackjack table or wait for the roulette wheel to stop spinning? But be careful not to lose it all in one night. If you're not a serious player, the slot machines are lots of fun, too. Strolling through the casinos people-watching is another great way to pass the time—weary gamblers desperately trying to claw back some of their losses, ecstatic cries of joy when their luck holds and the jangling of chips when the slots pay out.

Clockwise from top: The New Orleans-style House of Blues, Mandalay Bay Resort; cocktail bar, Mandalay Bay Resort; Studio 54 at the MGM Grand; you can enjoy a

show of all is free: walk The Strip after dark and be treated to the amazing performance of thousands of flashing neon lights.

From Highbrow to Fringe

With the ongoing regeneration of Downtown, a wider range of arts and culture is soon to add to the dazzling spectacle that is The Strip's traditional fare. Due to open in mid-2012 is The Smith Center, a major new architectural complex, which will house the Nevada Ballet Theatre and Las Vegas Philharmonic, and offer a program of world-class live performances. The fringe music scene is also alive and growing, with open-mike sessions and acoustic gigs at various venues, including The Beat and Emergency Arts (▷ 140) and The Arts Factory (▷ 66).

Discount Tickets

Top show tickets can cost upward of $100, but you can make big savings at discount agencies and in the free magazines. Tix4Tonight offers half-price tickets for same-day shows, with kiosks on The Strip; also Downtown at Four Queens Casino, Fremont Street; Mid-Strip at Circus Circus and Fashion Show Mall; and South Strip at the Showcase Mall next to the giant Coca-Cola bottle. Shows on offer are listed at 9.30 daily, with tickets on sale from 10–8, or tel 877/849-4868.

WEIRD AND WACKY

Las Vegas is constantly coming up with increasingly adventurous and sometimes edgy shows. Several hypnosis acts have volunteers from the audience live on stage to commit hilarious acts that border on the lewd, while Menopause: The Musical (▷ 70) dramatizes a subject most people of a certain age prefer to keep quiet about. Audience participation is ever popular: take front row seats at your peril. Subtle it ain't, but mainstream shows on The Strip are all about doing it loud and large.

cocktail any time of day or night; Rockhouse bar and nightclub attracts its fair share of celebrities; Le Rêve, Wynn Las Vegas

Directory

South Strip

Bars, Clubs and Lounges
Coyote Ugly
Mix Lounge
The Pub
Studio 54
Entertainment and Sports
Grand Garden Arena
Hollywood Theatre
The Lion King
Mandalay Bay Events Center
Soprano's Last Supper
Thomas & Mack Center/
  Sam Boyd Stadium
Golf
Bali Hai Golf Club
Music Venues
House of Blues
The Joint
LAX

Central Strip

Bars, Clubs and Lounges
Cleopatra's Barge
Ghostbar
Gordon-Biersch Las Vegas
Japonais
Napoleon's
Pure
V Bar

Entertainment and Sports
Blue Man Group
Colosseum
Flamingo Showroom
Improv Comedy Club
Penn and Teller
Phantom of the Opera
Theaters
UNLV Performing Arts Center
V Theater

North Strip

Bars, Clubs and Lounges
B Bar
Level 107 Lounge
Peppermill's Fire Side Lounge
Entertainment and Sports
Comedy Club
Las Vegas Hilton
Vegas Indoor Skydiving
Nightclubs
Tryst

Further Afield

Entertainment and Sports
Orleans Arena
Golf
Angel Park Golf Club
Las Vegas National
Royal Links Golf Club

Entertainment A-Z

ANGEL PARK GOLF CLUB

www.angelpark.com
Experience both mountains and palms at this 36-hole course designed by legendary golfer Arnold Palmer. There are spectacular views over Red Rock Canyon and the Las Vegas Valley.
✛ Off map ✉ 100 South Rampart Boulevard, west of US95 at Summerlin Parkway ☎ 702/254-4653 ◷ Daily (opening hours vary)

B BAR

www.wynnlasvegas.com
The B Bar, with a prime view of the casino floor, offers the perfect escape to indulge in nouvelle cocktails, fine wines, infused vodkas and spirits, before heading off to the adjacent baccarat room and casino for a flutter.
✛ D7–E7 ✉ Wynn Las Vegas, 3131 Las Vegas Boulevard South ☎ 702/770-7000 ◷ Daily 24 hours 🚌 Deuce

BALI HAI GOLF CLUB

www.balihaigolfclub.com

A South Pacific theme pervades throughout this 18-hole championship course off the southern end of The Strip, with outcrops of volcanic rock, groups of palm trees and white sand in the bunkers.

⊞ D12 ⊠ 5160 Las Vegas Boulevard South ☎ 702/597-2400 ⊙ Daily (opening hours vary) 🚌 Deuce; 104, 116

BLUE MAN GROUP

www.venetian.com

The most unusual show in Vegas has to be this group of guys with bright cobalt-blue bald heads, performing hilarious routines in which artistic canvases are created by the strangest means.

⊞ D8 ⊠ The Venetian, 3355 Las Vegas Boulevard South ☎ 702/414-1000 ⊙ Daily 7pm and 10pm 🚌 Deuce 👋 Very expensive

CLEOPATRA'S BARGE

www.caesarspalace.com

This floating club is a replica of the vessel that carried the Egyptian Queen Cleopatra along the Nile. During the week, a DJ plays contemporary dance music, and there's live music on weekends.

⊞ C8–D8 ⊠ Caesars Palace, 3570 Las Vegas Boulevard South ☎ 702/731-7110 ⊙ Daily, bar from noon, entertainment from 9pm till late 🚌 Deuce

COLOSSEUM

www.caesarspalace.com

This magnificent auditorium has been purpose-built to stage extravaganzas, and features international superstars. Celine Dion is returning here for another three-year run from 2011.

⊞ C8–D8 ⊠ Caesars Palace, 3570 Las Vegas Boulevard South ☎ 702/731-7110 ⊙ Daily (show times vary) 🚌 Deuce

COMEDY CLUB

www.rivierahotel.com

Four acts a night do stand-up at this comedy spot on the second floor of the Mardi Gras Plaza at the Riviera. Once a month the venue holds a late-night show for X-rated comedians.

⊞ E6–E7 ⊠ Riviera, 2901 Las Vegas Boulevard South ☎ 702/794-9433 ⊙ Daily (show times vary) 🚌 Deuce

COYOTE UGLY

www.coyoteuglysaloon.com

If you enjoyed the movie or have visited the New York original, you'll love the Las Vegas version of one of the most famous bars in the country. It's a fun Southern-style saloon with bartenders who dance on the bar. Founder Lillian Lovell perfectly summed up her bar's ethos when she said "Serving cheap tequila from a boot, bartending with boa constrictors and just doing whatever the hell

---

TICKET INFORMATION

The popular long-running shows and the new ones sell out quickly, so it's advisable to make reservations. Call the relevant hotel or check out its website, which will have a reservation facility. Otherwise, shows can be reserved through TicketMaster (www.ticketmaster.com). Reservations are taken for long-running shows up to 30 days in advance; limited-time concerts or sporting events such as boxing matches can be reserved three months in advance. Note that shows can close with little notice so it is always best to check to avoid disappointment.

Where there's a casino, there's a lounge or bar

I wanted are what made the Coyote great."

➕ D10 ✉ New York-New York, 3790 Las Vegas Boulevard South ☎ 702/740-6330 🕐 Daily 6pm–late 🚌 Deuce

FLAMINGO SHOWROOM

www.flamingolasvegas.com

Founded in the 1940s and formerly owned by Mob legend Bugsy Siegel, the Flamingo has long had a high reputation for hosting show business legends—Nat King Cole and Jerry Lewis have graced the stage here. Currently, Donny and Marie Osmond—still smiling broadly—are top of the bill here, plus stand-up comedian George Wallace and magician Nathan Burton.

➕ D9 ✉ Flamingo, 3555 Las Vegas Boulevard South ☎ 702/733-3333 🕐 Daily (show times vary) 🚌 Deuce

GHOSTBAR

www.palms.com

One of Vegas's most talked about bars, with a simple, yet eclectic look, is atop the Palms Hotel. Marvel at the breathtaking views from 55 floors up while music from the DJ fills the background. From the outside deck is yet another fantastic view, one from a glass floor looking directly down at the Palms Pool below. A young and trendy crowd mix with the celebrity clientele.

➕ A9 ✉ Palms, 4321 Flamingo Road ☎ 702/942-6832 🕐 Daily 8pm–4am 🚌 202

GORDON-BIERSCH LAS VEGAS

www.gordonbiersch.com

Exposed pipes and gleaming brewing equipment set the stage for this hangout, popular with local yuppies. The beers include tasty German brews that are changed seasonally.

➕ F8 ✉ 3987 Paradise Road ☎ 702/312-5247 🕐 Fri–Sat 11am–1am, Sun–Thu 11am–midnight 🚌 108

GRAND GARDEN ARENA

www.mgmgrand.com

This is one of the biggest venues in town, hosting huge events ranging from top entertainers to world championship boxing.

Tickets can be bought up to two months in advance.
✚ D10 ✉ MGM Grand, 3799 Las Vegas Boulevard South ☎ 702/891-1111 🕐 Daily (show times vary) 🚌 Deuce

HOLLYWOOD THEATRE

www.mgmgrand.com
MGM's smaller, more intimate, venue hosts internationally acclaimed shows and a variety of world-class performers, including Tom Jones and David Copperfield, and also puts on top-line comedy acts.
✚ D10 ✉ MGM Grand, 3799 Las Vegas Boulevard South ☎ 702/891-7777 🕐 Daily (show times vary) 🚌 Deuce

HOUSE OF BLUES

www.mandalaybay.com
Bringing New Orleans to Las Vegas, this superb, 1,500-seat venue is on three levels and features such big-name stars as B. B. King and Brian Ferry. There's great food, including the popular Sunday Gospel Brunch. Check out the unusual artworks, too.
✚ D11 ✉ Mandalay Bay, 3950 Las Vegas Boulevard South ☎ 702/632-7607 🕐 Daily (show times vary) 🚌 Deuce

IMPROV COMEDY CLUB

www.harrahs.com
Two comedy shows a night (except Monday) feature emerging stars from a branch of the famous Improv comedy club. The production is professional, the theater is small and cozy, and the comedians usually give a good mix of set routines, improvization and topical banter.
✚ D8 ✉ Harrah's, 3475 Las Vegas Boulevard South ☎ 702/369-5111 🕐 Tue–Sun 8.30 and 10.30pm 🚌 Deuce

JAPONAIS

www.themirage.com
Relax in this exotic lounge amid tropical foliage and lulled by the soothing sound of waterfalls as you dine on sushi and sip cocktails.
✚ C8–D8 ✉ The Mirage, 3400 Las Vegas Boulevard South ☎ 702/792-7979 🕐 Fri–Sat 2pm–2am, Sun–Thu 2pm–midnight 🚌 Deuce

THE JOINT

www.hardrockhotel.com
One of Vegas' hottest venues, with a capacity of 1,400, The Joint features super DJ Tiesto and cutting-edge bands worthy of the Hard Rock image.
✚ F9 ✉ Hard Rock Hotel, 4455 Paradise Road ☎ 702/693-4000 🕐 Daily (show times vary) 🚌 108

LAS VEGAS HILTON

www.lvhilton.com
A variety of musicians, comedians and magicians perform here and

DRESS CODES

Most, if not all, of the nightclubs listed here impose quite a strict dress code, so it's a good idea to check what is acceptable beforehand. Men will have more trouble than women when it comes to what they are wearing: jeans and sneakers are guaranteed to keep hopefuls out of any club. Women are also more likely than men to get in when there are long lines. You can get onto the VIP list if you know someone who works at the club, or if you have spent a lot in the casino. Otherwise, join the line outside the door (about an hour before opening time at the most popular places) and hope for the best. Cover charges, where they exist, are usually less than $20, and may be at different rates for men and women.

CIRQUE DU SOLEIL

This troupe, originally from Quebec in Canada, has taken circus arts to new levels with its breathtaking skills and supremely artistic concept shows. It has won over Las Vegas, with several shows currently running: Mystère at Treasure Island (Sat–Wed); "O" at Bellagio (Wed–Sun); Zumanity at New York-New York (Fri–Sun, Tue–Wed); Kà at MGM Grand (Tue–Sat); The Beatles: LOVE at The Mirage (▷ 66); Criss Angel: Believe at Luxor (Tue–Sat). For further details tel 702/796-9999; www.cirquedusoleil.com

tickets are reasonably priced. The three venues offer a choice of big shows in the Hilton Theater, comedy in the Shimmer Cabaret, and music and live entertainment in the über-chic Tempo Lounge.

➕ F7 ✉ Las Vegas Hilton, 3000 Paradise Road ☎ 702/732-5755 ⏰ Daily (opening hours vary) 🚌 108

LAS VEGAS NATIONAL

www.lasvegasnational.com
Opened in 1961, this classic 18-hole golf course has glistening lakes. In 1996, champion golfer Tiger Woods won his first PGA victory here, and over the years the course has hosted many top-class tournaments.

➕ J7–J8 ✉ 1911 Desert Inn Road ☎ 702/734-1796 ⏰ Daily (opening hours vary) 🚌 213

LAX

www.laxthenightclub.com
This huge two-story space with dramatic spiral staircases, oversized mirrors and chandeliers, and fabulous decor attracts a cool, discerning young crowd, A-list celebrities and the social jet set. Top DJs play from a raised platform through an unrivaled sound system to the swanky dance floor below.

➕ C11–D11 ✉ Luxor, 3900 Las Vegas Boulevard South ☎ 702/262-4529 ⏰ Wed–Sat 10pm–4am 🚌 Deuce

LEVEL 107 LOUNGE

www.stratospherehotel.com
Visit this sophisticated lounge bar before or after a meal at the Top of the World restaurant (▷ 149). High up on the 107th floor, it has great city views. You can sip a cocktail in the intimate surroundings while listening to live music and relaxing in the snazzy leopard and leather chairs.

➕ E5–F5 ✉ Stratosphere, 2000 Las Vegas Boulevard South ☎ 702/380-7705 ⏰ Daily from 4pm till late 🚌 Deuce

THE LION KING

www.mandalaybay.com
Opened May 2009, The Lion King is the first Disney production to play in this gambling Mecca (a gamble in itself). The show reigns as one of the most popular productions around the globe, and the Mandalay Bay's version follows this successful format, with all of the same spectacular music, sets and costumes. It's an amazing show.

➕ D11 ✉ Mandalay Bay, 3950 Las Vegas Boulevard South ☎ 702/632-7777 ⏰ Mon–Thu 8pm, Sat–Sun 4 and 8pm 🚌 Deuce 💲 Very expensive

MANDALAY BAY EVENTS CENTER

www.mandalaybay.com
This major venue seats 12,000 and hosts big-name concerts and

major sporting events. On one night, usually in June, it is transformed into a gigantic nightclub for the "Summer of Love" event.

🔲 D11 ✉ Mandalay Bay, 3950 Las Vegas Boulevard South ☎ 702/632-7777 🕐 Daily (show times vary) 🚌 Deuce

MIX LOUNGE

www.mandalaybay.com

Mix a seductive blend of music played by savvy DJs, great cocktails, an innovative bar menu, tasty tapas and breathtaking views from 64 floors up and you have one of the most stylish and fashionable hotspots on The Strip. Reserve a table indoors or go out on the balcony. DJs Frankie 808 and Myk spin a mix of hip-hop, house and other contemporary sounds. Admission is free to hotel guests and local ladies.

🔲 D11 ✉ Mandalay Bay, 3950 Las Vegas Boulevard South ☎ 702/632-9500 🕐 Daily 5pm–late 🚌 Deuce

Penn and Teller at the Rio

NAPOLEON'S

www.parislasvegas.com

The French theme at this champagne bar incorporates over 100 varieties of the world's finest champagnes, and French-style hot and cold appetizers. Note: if you sit near the dueling pianists you may very well become part of their comic routine!

🔲 D9 ✉ Paris Las Vegas, 3655 Las Vegas Boulevard South ☎ 702/946-7000 🕐 Show nightly at 9pm 🚌 Deuce

ORLEANS ARENA

www.orleansarena.com

Since opening in 2004, this huge arena has hosted Disney on Ice, top concerts and a variety of sporting events.

🔲 A10 ✉ Orleans, 4500 West Tropicana ☎ 702/365-SHOW; tickets 702/284-7777 🕐 Daily (show times vary) 🚌 201

PENN AND TELLER

www.riolasvegas.com

This talented, eccentric partnership combines magic, illusions, juggling, comedy and stunts in an intelligent show. They have been together for over 30 years: Penn is big, loud and talkative, while Teller is whimsically mute.

🔲 B8 ✉ Rio, 3700 West Flamingo Road ☎ 702/777-7776 🕐 Daily 9pm 🚌 202 💵 Very expensive

PEPPERMILL'S FIRE SIDE LOUNGE

www.peppermilllasvegas.com

Shag carpeting, fire pits, enormous white silk flowers and indoor fountains are still the rage at this tribute to old-world Vegas.

🔲 E7 ✉ 2985 Las Vegas Boulevard South ☎ 702/735-4177 🕐 Daily 24 hours 🚌 Deuce

Headliners come and go in the city, some staying longer than others, but Las Vegas likes to keep its future big names under wraps, so you never know what's lined up. Recent superstars who have performed here include U2, Paul McCartney and Barry Manilow. As shows can close just like that, it is always best to check before turning up.

PHANTOM OF THE OPERA

www.phantomlasvegas.com
Andrew Lloyd Webber's famous musical phenomenon opened in 2006 in the majestic grandeur of the Venetian and continues to enthrall its audiences.

➕ D8 ✉ The Venetian, 3355 Las Vegas Boulevard South ☎ 702/414-9000 🕐 Mon–Sat 7pm (also 9.30pm Tue, Sat) 🚌 Deuce 💷 Very expensive

THE PUB

www.montecarlo.com
After extensive modification, out go the huge copper barrels that typified the Monte Carlo Brew Pub and in comes a new contemporary look and a new name to go with it.

➕ D10 ✉ Monte Carlo, 3770 Las Vegas Boulevard South ☎ 702/730-7777 🕐 Sun–Thu 11–11, Fri–Sat 11am–3am 🚌 Deuce

PURE

www.caesarspalace.com
This sumptuous and sexy nightclub, high up in Caesars Palace, has four venues all giving great views over The Strip and each with its own DJ playing the top chart hits.

➕ C8–D8 ✉ Caesars Palace, 3570 Las Vegas Boulevard South ☎ 702/731-7833 🕐 Tue, Thu–Sun 10pm–late 🚌 Deuce

ROYAL LINKS GOLF CLUB

www.royallinksgolfclub.com
This course has holes based on those from famous British Open courses, including St. Andrews, Royal Troon, Carnoustie and Turnberry. The 18th hole looks like a medieval castle.

➕ Off map ✉ 5995 East Vegas Valley Road, 6 miles (10km) east ☎ 702/450-8123 🕐 Daily (opening hours vary)

SOPRANO'S LAST SUPPER

www.sopranoslastsupper.com
There's plenty of action, singing and dancing and a first-class Italian dinner to indulge in at this interactive spoof on the famous hit TV series, *The Sopranos*, but don't expect to stay in your seat all evening.

➕ D10 ✉ Tropicana, 3801 Las Vegas Boulevard South ☎ 702/733-8669; 800/829-9034 🕐 Shows Tue–Sun 7pm 🚌 Deuce

STUDIO 54

www.mgmgrand.com
Popular with celebrities, this hot, high-energy club is a replica of the 1970s original in New York, with state-of-the-art sound, video and lighting.

➕ D10 ✉ MGM Grand, 3799 Las Vegas Boulevard South ☎ 702/891-7254 🕐 Tue–Sat 10pm–late 🚌 Deuce

THOMAS & MACK CENTER/ SAM BOYD STADIUM

www.unlvtickets.com
This state-of-the-art, multi-purpose arena stages world-class entertainment and major national sports events, and has a seating capacity of 19,511. Events range from monster truck racing, boxing and show jumping to music

concerts, rodeo, basketball and ice shows.

G10 ✉ University of Nevada, 4505 South Maryland Parkway ☎ 702/895-3761 🕐 Daily (show times vary) 🚌 109

TRYST

www.wynnlasvegas.com

Rapidly becoming one of the most enticing nightclubs in the city, Tryst sets a new trend for nightlife in Las Vegas. Sophisticated deep-red and black combinations enhance intimate booth-style seating and the open-air dance floor extends into a 90ft (27m) waterfall that cascades into a lagoon.

🔲 D7–E7 ✉ Wynn Las Vegas, 3131 Las Vegas Boulevard South ☎ 702/770-3375 🕐 Thu–Sat 10pm–4am 🚌 Deuce

UNLV PERFORMING ARTS CENTER

http://pac.unlv.edu

See major international artists perform classical and popular music, dance, theater, ballet and opera. The center comprises the Artemus W. Ham Concert Hall (home to the Nevada Symphony Orchestra), the Judy Bayley Theater and the Black Box Theater.

🔲 G9 ✉ University of Nevada, 4505 South Maryland Parkway ☎ 702/895-3535 🕐 Daily (show times vary) 🚌 109

V BAR

www.venetian.com

Enclosed in opaque glass walls, this high-roller's joint oozes sophistication. Sleek lines, leather chaise longues and subdued lighting enhance the atmosphere.

🔲 D8 ✉ The Venetian, 3355 Las Vegas Boulevard South ☎ 702/414-1000 🕐 Thu–Sat 5pm–3am, Sun–Wed 5pm–2am 🚌 Deuce

V THEATER

www.varietytheater.com

This specially tailored venue, which includes private sections, showcases a varied program during the day and evening, from comedy, variety and magic to game shows and tribute acts.

🔲 D9 ✉ Miracle Mile, 3663 Las Vegas Boulevard South ☎ 702/892-7792 🕐 Daily (show times vary) 🚌 Deuce

VEGAS INDOOR SKYDIVING

www.vegasindoorskydiving.com

Test your skills at this exciting new sporting challenge. A vertical wind tunnel simulates the free-fall experience of skydiving in a column of air, with vertical airspeeds up to 120mph (193kph). No experience is needed; you can book a single flight session or a personalized coaching program.

🔲 F7 ✉ 200 Convention Center Drive ☎ 702/770-3384 🕐 Daily 9.45–8 🚌 108, Deuce

Simulated skydiving in a wind tunnel

Eat

There are places to eat across the city to suit all tastes and budgets. In this section establishments are listed alphabetically.

EAT

Introduction

Not formerly renowned for good cuisine, Las Vegas has turned things around from the days of lining up for a buffet that focused on quantity rather than quality.

So What's on Offer?

For starters, the famous Vegas buffet has become much more exciting and provides something for everyone at a reasonable price. There are endless top-class establishments where you can feast on the superb cuisine of Michelin-star chefs and there's also the opportunity to dine at a restaurant run by a celebrity chef. The sheer variety of cuisine that has emerged is astonishing, from Italian and Mexican to Mediterranean, Indian and Pacific Rim. Fast-food outlets still play an important role, as do traditional steak houses.

Dining Tips

It can be hard to get a table at high-end restaurants, especially on Friday and Saturday nights. Plan ahead—you can reserve up to 30 days in advance. Many of these open for dinner only. Mid-range eateries are more likely to be open all day, and you will not need a reservation for breakfast or lunch. Most major hotels have a fast-food court to grab a quick bite, and many have a buffet at breakfast, lunch and dinner. Buffet lines can be long, so allow plenty of time.

DINNER SHOWS

If your time is short in Las Vegas take advantage of one of the dinner shows on offer, where you can eat and be thoroughly entertained at the same time. Probably the most popular of these is Tournament of Kings at the Excalibur (▷ 29), where you meal is accompanied by a jousting tournament, dragons, wizards and great special effects. Also making headlines is Tony n' Tina's Wedding (▷ 73) a wild-and-wacky show in which you are invited to join Tony and Tina for their wedding feast.

In the last few years the dining scene in Las Vegas has reached new heights of excellence and glamour with the arrival of world-famous chefs and celebrity owners

EAT

Directory

South Strip

Buffets
Bayside Buffet
Cafés
Il Fornaio Panetteria
Verandah High Tea
French and Other European
Joël Robuchon
Red Square
International
Cathouse
North American and Mexican
Aureole
Border Grill
Emeril's
Toto's
Oriental/Fusion
China Grill
Fleur
Noodle Shop
Steaks and Seafood
Charlie Palmer Steak
Craftsteak
Nobhill Tavern

Central Strip

Buffets
Bellagio Buffet
Carnival World
Paradise Garden Buffet
Cafés
Harley Davidson Café
Jean-Philippe Patisserie
French and Other European
Bouchon
Mon Ami Gabi
Picasso
International
Pampas Brazilian Grille
Italian
Battista's Hole in the Wall
Canaletto
Francesco's
Valentino
North American and Mexican
Bradley Ogden
Dos Caminos

Mesa Grill
Postrio
Strip House
Oriental/Fusion
Hyakumi
Koi
Kokomo's
Steaks and Seafood
Lawry's The Prime Rib
Michael Mina
Nero's
Village Seafood

North Strip

French and Other European
Top of the World
International
DJT
Italian
Piero's
North American and Mexican
Johnny Rocket's
Oriental/Fusion
Lotus of Siam
Ra
Steaks and Seafood
Envy
Kristofer's
The Steak House

Downtown

Buffets
Garden Court
Cafés
The Beat
Binion's Café
French and Other European
Hugo's Cellar
North American and Mexican
Doña Maria Tamales
Oriental/Fusion
Lillie's Noodle House
Second Street Grill
Steaks and Seafood
Binion's Ranch Steakhouse
Triple George Grill

EAT

Eating A-Z

PRICES

Prices are approximate, based on a 3-course meal for one person.

$$$	over $50
$$	$20–$50
$	under $20

AUREOLE $$$

www.mandalaybay.com

This restaurant has big windows, glass-covered waterfalls and a massive award-winning wine tower, holding 10,000-plus bottles. American meat and seafood dishes dominate the first-class menu here.

🔲 D11 ✉ Mandalay Bay, 3950 Las Vegas Boulevard South ☎ 702/632-7401 ⏰ Daily 5.30–10.30pm 🚍 Deuce

BATTISTA'S HOLE IN THE WALL $$

www.battistaslasvegas.com

For more than 30 years people have been flocking here for the excellent Italian food, served with style.

You can count on service with a smile

🔲 D9 ✉ 4041 Audrie Street ☎ 702/732-1424 ⏰ Daily 5–10.30pm 🚍 Deuce

BAYSIDE BUFFET $$

www.mandalaybay.com

Floor-to-ceiling windows here give sweeping views of the tropical lagoon outside. Although the buffet is not over-large, the cuisine is very good, with excellent salads, hearty meats and one of the better dessert selections, all made on the premises.

🔲 D11 ✉ Mandalay Bay, 3950 Las Vegas Boulevard South ☎ 702/632-7402 ⏰ Daily 7–2.30, 4.45–10 🚍 Deuce

THE BEAT $

www.thebeatlv.com

This delightfully laidback, arty café inside the Emergency Arts gallery has books and magazines to read, secondhand LPs for sale and live music nightly. Great breakfasts, creative sandwiches (Slap and Tickle: organic peanut butter and homemade jam with smoked bacon on *pain de mie*), salads and soups are served by the friendly and chatty staff. It's excellent value for money and very popular.

🔲 G3 ✉ 520 Fremont Street, Downtown ☎ 702/409-5563 ⏰ Mon–Fri 9am–midnight, Sun 9–3 🚍 108, Deuce

BELLAGIO BUFFET $$

More expensive than most buffets, this is probably the most highly regarded. It has many different types of cuisine, including Italian, Chinese and Japanese, all served in a European marketplace-style setting.

🔲 C9–D9 ✉ Bellagio, 3600 Las Vegas Boulevard South ☎ 702/693-7111 ⏰ Daily 7am–10pm 🚍 Deuce

BINION'S CAFÉ $

www.binions.com

If you're looking for a great place for a light snack or something more substantial at a low price, you should try this simple no-frills café. The generous breakfasts are particularly good.

🔳 G3 ☒ Binion's, 128 East Fremont Street ☎ 702/382-1600 🕐 Mon–Thu 24 hours, Fri–Sun 10am–7am 🚌 108, Deuce

BINION'S RANCH STEAKHOUSE $$$

www.binions.com

Settle down to the delicious succulent steaks and chops that are served amid the attractive Victorian decor, while taking in the spectacular views of Las Vegas.

🔳 G3 ☒ Binion's, 128 East Fremont Street ☎ 702/382-1600 🕐 Daily 5.30–10.30pm 🚌 108, Deuce

BORDER GRILL $$

www.mandalaybay.com

Come here for great Mexican home cooking in a lively setting. Lunch on spicy baby back ribs on the patio or get a take-out taco.

🔳 D11 ☒ Mandalay Bay, 3950 Las Vegas Boulevard South ☎ 702/632-7403 🕐 Mon–Thu 11.30–10, Fri 11.30–11, Sat 11–11, Sun 11–10 🚌 Deuce

BOUCHON $$

www.bouchonbistro.com

World-renowned chef Thomas Keller showcases his bistro fare, delighting both the palate and the eye, at Bouchon, located in the Venetian Tower. Deep blue velvet seating, antique lights, a mosaic floor and hand-painted murals provide a sophisticated café-style ambience amid an enchanting poolside garden.

🔳 D8 ☒ The Venetian 3355 Las Vegas Boulevard South ☎ 702/414-6200 🕐 Daily 7–10.30, 5–10, also Sat–Sun 8–2 🚌 Deuce

BRADLEY OGDEN $$$

www.caesarspalace.com

This famed San Francisco chef has earned national acclaim for his classic, fresh American cooking. Polished floors and dark wood give a sleek look to the elegant and refined dining room where serious, quality food is served by first-class professional staff.

🔳 C8–D8 ☒ Caesars Palace, 3570 Las Vegas Boulevard South ☎ 877/346-4642 🕐 Tue–Sun 5–11pm 🚌 Deuce

CANALETTO $$$

www.venetian.com

Where better to sample good northern Italian cuisine than on a re-creation of Venice's St. Mark's Square? Some little-known Italian wines are on offer to complement your meal.

🔳 D8 ☒ The Venetian, 3355 Las Vegas Boulevard South ☎ 702/733-0070 🕐 Sun–Thu 11.30–11, Fri–Sat 11.30–midnight 🚌 Deuce

EAT

LESS IS MORE

The latest trend around town is to offer "sliders"—mini versions of main course dishes, and tapas as appetizers. These are great alternatives if you're not ravenously hungry or are in a group and want to share. Typical sliders are mini-burgers, served for instance at KGB (Harrah's, 3475 Las Vegas Boulevard South), as well as Fleur (▷ 143), and you can get some great tapas-style tortillas and tacos at the Mesa Grill (▷ 146) in Caesars Palace.

Apart from the fast-food establishments selling hot dogs, burgers and pizzas, Las Vegas has many more options to prevent your kids from going hungry. Buffets enable them to pick and choose what they like, and most have an ice-cream machine that you can use to blackmail them into eating their greens. Theme restaurants children will love include the Rainforest Café at the MGM Grand (✉ 3799 Las Vegas Boulevard South ☎ 702/891-8580; www.rainforestcafe.com ⏰ Sun–Thu 8am–11pm, Fri–Sat 8am–midnight), with jungle foliage, waterfalls, robotic animals and thunderstorms.

CARNIVAL WORLD $$

www.riolasvegas.com

This is one of the best buffets in Las Vegas, with chefs cooking on view at various points around the serving islands. There are 11 styles of cuisine on offer, from Brazilian to Mongolian.

➕ B8 ✉ Rio, 3700 West Flamingo Road ☎ 702/777-7777 ⏰ Daily 8am–10pm 🚌 202

CATHOUSE $$

www.cathouselv.com

This classy hybrid of a seductive restaurant orchestrated by celebrity chef Kerry Simon, and Burlesque-style lounge, has an eclectic menu of shared small-plate fusion dishes.

➕ C11–D11 ✉ Luxor, 3900 Las Vegas Boulevard South ☎ 702/262-4000 ⏰ Daily 6–11pm 🚌 Deuce

CHARLIE PALMER STEAK $$$

www.fourseasons.com/lasvegas

Subdued gleaming woodwork, bronze wall sculptures and an exclusive atmosphere set the scene for a meal that might include charcoal-grilled filet mignon or steamed halibut.

➕ D11 ✉ Four Seasons, 3960 Las Vegas Boulevard South ☎ 702/632-5000 ⏰ Daily 5.30–10.30pm 🚌 Deuce

CHINA GRILL $$

www.mandalaybay.com

Come with a group of friends or family and prepare to splurge on the massive portions served up in this imaginative Asian restaurant.

➕ D11 ✉ Mandalay Bay, 3950 Las Vegas Boulevard South ☎ 702/632-7404 ⏰ Daily 5.30pm–midnight 🚌 Deuce

CRAFTSTEAK $$$

www.mgmgrand.com

Beautifully prepared hand-selected beef from small farms and artisan producers is served here.

➕ D10 ✉ MGM Grand, 3799 Las Vegas Boulevard South ☎ 702/891-7318 ⏰ Sun–Thu 5.30–10pm, Fri 5.30–10.30pm, Sat 5–10.30pm 🚌 Deuce

DJT $$$

www.trumplasvegashotel.com

Named after the initials of the Trump Hotel's illustrious owner, Donald J. Trump, this restaurant offers fine dishes crafted by chef Joseph Isidori.

➕ D7 ✉ 2000 Fashion Show Drive ☎ 702/982-0000 ⏰ Breakfast daily 6.30–11, lunch daily 11.30–2, dinner Tue–Sun 5–10 🚌 Deuce

DONA MARIA TAMALES $

www.donamariatamales.com

The best dishes are the great tamales; shredded chicken, beef and pork wrapped in cornmeal.

➕ G4 ✉ 910 Las Vegas Boulevard South ☎ 702/382-6538 ⏰ Mon–Fri 8am–10pm, Sat–Sun 8am–11pm 🚌 Deuce

DOS CAMINOS $$–$$$

www.brguestrestaurants.com

Dos Caminos delights with its authentic, innovative Mexican cuisine, such as classic staples: *empanada* and *frijoles borrachos* ("drunken beans"). They serve a mean *cochinita pibil* (slow-roasted suckling pig), so tender it falls apart at a touch of the fork. The surroundings are equally inventive: shimmering copper glass and gold and fuchsia tiles on the wall.

➕ D8 ✉ The Palazzo, 3325 Las Vegas Boulevard South ☎ 702/577-9600
🕐 Daily 11–11 🚌 Deuce

EMERIL'S $$$

www.mgmgrand.com

This is a re-creation of Emeril Lagasse's New Orleans restaurant, specializing in spicy Creole/Cajun recipes. The menu includes barbecued shrimp, veal sirloin and sumptuous banana cream pie drizzled with caramel.

➕ D10 ✉ MGM Grand, 3799 Las Vegas Boulevard South ☎ 702/891-1111
🕐 Daily 11–2.30, 5–10 🚌 Deuce

ENVY $$$

www.envysteakhouse.com

Richard Chamberlain, one of America's leading chefs, uses top-quality fresh ingredients in his innovative dishes, which redefine the traditional steak-house offerings. Soothing red shades give a sophisticated feel.

➕ F7 ✉ Renaissance, 3400 Paradise Road ☎ 702/784-5716 🕐 Daily 6.30–2, 5–10
🚌 108

FLEUR $$$

www.mandalaybay.com

Celebrity chef Hubert Keller serves bold and fun American-Asian fusion cuisine in Fleur's informal modern setting. Nibble on parmesan paprika popcorn or blow your budget on the $5,000 FleurBurger: wagyu minced beef, foie gras, and truffles, washed down with a bottle of 1995 Chateau Petrus. There are also vegetarian and organic options, with small tapas-style dishes ideal for sharing.

➕ D11 ✉ Mandalay Bay, 3950 Las Vegas Boulevard South ☎ 702/632-9400
🕐 Daily 11–3, 5–11 🚌 Deuce

IL FORNAIO PANETTERIA $

www.nynyhotelcasino.com

It's worth making a special journey to this Italian bakery café just for its espresso-mocha scones with chocolate chunks.

➕ D10 ✉ New York-New York, 3790 Las Vegas Boulevard South ☎ 702/740-6403
🕐 Daily 7.30am–midnight 🚌 Deuce

FRANCESCO'S $$

www.treasureisland.com

Superb Neapolitan pizza and pastas and delectable desserts are served at this friendly restaurant. Good house wines are sold by the carafe.

BUFFET KNOW-HOW

Buffets offer breakfast, lunch and dinner, with a different range of food available at each meal. They are a great option for families, particularly those that include fussy eaters, because there is sure to be something for everyone. Buffets also offer tremendous value for the money. This does, of course, mean that they are popular and lines can be long, especially at peak times. At the most popular buffets, you may need to allow up to three hours for your meal.

EAT

🚉 D8 ⊠ Treasure Island, 3300 Las Vegas
Boulevard South ☎ 702/894-7111
🕐 Sun–Thu 11am–2am, Fri–Sat 11am–1am
🚌 Deuce

GARDEN COURT $

www.mainstreetcasino.com

Watch your food being prepared
for you at what is said to be
Downtown's best buffet. Choices
include Mexican, Asian and
American, plus specialty nights
such as T-bone Tuesday.

🚉 G2 ⊠ Main Street Station, 200 North
Main Street ☎ 702/387-1896 🕐 Daily
7am–10pm 🚌 108, Deuce

HARLEY DAVIDSON CAFÉ $

www.harley-davidsoncafe.com

Motorcycle buffs will enthuse over
this American roadside café. Many
gleaming machines are on display,
including one owned by Elvis, and
memorabilia covers the walls. Try
the tollhouse-cookie pie.

🚉 D9 ⊠ 3725 Las Vegas Boulevard South
☎ 702/740-4555 🕐 Sun–Thu 11am–
midnight, Fri–Sat 11am–2am 🚌 Deuce

HUGO'S CELLAR $$$

www.hugoscellar.com

Below street level, this romantic
restaurant has a touch of class.
Each woman receives a red rose
as she enters the low-lit, dark-
wood space. There's excellent
Continental cuisine and some

dishes are prepared at the table.
Expect lots of pampering.

🚉 G3 ⊠ Four Queens Hotel, 202 Fremont
Street ☎ 702/385-4011 🕐 Daily
5–10.30pm 🚌 108, Deuce

HYAKUMI $$

www.caesarspalace.com

Teppanyaki chefs at this Japanese
restaurant and sushi bar prepare
your meal at your table with great
flair and entertainment value.
There's a good range of sake and
Japanese beers, too.

🚉 C8–D8 ⊠ Caesars Palace, 3570 Las
Vegas Boulevard South ☎ 877/346-4642
🕐 Daily 11–3, 5–11 🚌 Deuce

JEAN-PHILIPPE PATISSERIE $

www.arialasvegas.com

This chic little café serves cakes
and pastries that are almost too
pretty to eat, and possibly the best
croque-monsieur in town. Its
adjacent shop sells gourmet
chocolates.

🚉 C10 ⊠ ARIA Resort and Casino, 3730
Las Vegas Boulevard South ☎ 877/230-
2742 🕐 Daily 6am–midnight 🚌 Deuce

JOËL ROBUCHON $$$

www.mgmgrand.com

Robuchon's reputation for the
highest standards is upheld here
at the MGM. The sophisticated
16-course menu is an experience,
or if you prefer a scaled-down

EATING ON A BUDGET

If you are on a tight budget you have several options for eating inexpensively. So long as
you keep playing, most casinos will ply you with free food and drink—though take care not
to spend more than you save. There are plenty of well-known fast-food chains on The Strip,
if all you want is to refuel on the go. Try the various ethnic food courts, such as Las Vegas
Chinatown Plaza (▷ 120), and others beyond The Strip, like the Colonnade Mall on
Southeastern Avenue. Many informal restaurants, such as the Peppermill, at 2985 Las Vegas
Boulevard South, serve large portions, and are happy to provide doggy bags.

version, choose the six-course tasting menu.

⊞ D10 ⊠ MGM Grand, 3799 Las Vegas Boulevard South ☎ 702/891-7925 ⏰ Sun–Thu 5.30–10pm, Fri–Sat 5.30–10.30pm 🚌 Deuce

JOHNNY ROCKET'S $

www.thefashionshow.com
The waitresses at this American retro diner, which serves burgers, club sandwiches, great malts and shakes, line up and dance every half hour.

⊞ D7 ⊠ Fashion Show Mall, 3200 Las Vegas Boulevard South ☎ 702/731-5614 ⏰ Mon–Sat 10–9, Sun 11–7 🚌 Deuce

KOI $$$

www.koirestaurant.com
This outpost of the New York hotspot exudes a sophisticated tone. Koi cooks up modern and traditional Japanese-inspired dishes with a Californian accent; try the Chilean sea bass and Kobe filet mignon, with one of the best views of the Bellagio fountains.

⊞ D9 ⊠ Planet Hollywood, 3667 Las Vegas Boulevard South ☎ 702/454-4555 ⏰ Sun–Thu 5.30–10.30pm, Fri–Sat 5.30–11.30pm 🚌 Deuce

KOKOMO'S $$

www.themirage.com
Tropical surroundings complement the delicious Hawaiian cuisine, including fish with broiled bananas and coconut shrimp.

⊞ C8–D8 ⊠ The Mirage, 3400 Las Vegas Boulevard South ☎ 702/791-7111 ⏰ Daily 5–10.30pm 🚌 Deuce

KRISTOFER'S $$

www.rivierahotel.com
The great steaks, tender ribs and broiled chicken in butter served

The Harley Davidson Café

here are matched by great prices; the barbecue sauce is wonderful.

⊞ E6–E7 ⊠ Riviera, 2901 Las Vegas Boulevard South ☎ 702/794-9233 ⏰ Daily 5.30–10pm 🚌 Deuce

LAWRY'S THE PRIME RIB $$$

www.lawrysonline.com
Lawry's is popular for its perfectly cooked, tasty prime rib, which is carved at the table. Waitresses in stylish uniforms and starched white caps tend to your every need in the art deco surroundings.

⊞ E9 ⊠ 4043 Howard Hughes Parkway ☎ 702/893-2223 ⏰ Mon–Fri 11.30–2, Sun–Thu 5–10pm, Fri–Sat 5–11pm 🚌 202

LILLIE'S NOODLE HOUSE $$

www.goldennugget.com
There's an odd mix of cultures at work here, but the cuisine is mostly Chinese, and the Sichuan and Cantonese dishes are of exceptional quality. Japanese dishes served on teppanyaki hot griddles add another taste.

⊞ G3 ⊠ Golden Nugget, 129 East Fremont Street ☎ 702/385-7111 ⏰ Daily 5pm–midnight 🚌 108, Deuce

LOTUS OF SIAM $

www.saipinchutima.com

Lotus of Siam is one of only a few Thai restaurants in Las Vegas, with a huge menu of dishes. Let them know how hot you like your food and they'll prepare it accordingly. If you overdo it, have the coconut ice cream for dessert.

🚰 G6 ⊠ 953 East Sahara Avenue ☎ 702/735-3033 🕔 Mon–Fri 11.30–2.30, 5.30–9.30, Sat–Sun 5.30–10pm 🚌 204

MESA GRILL $$

www.caesarspalace.com

Sample adventurous modern US Southwestern-Mexican fusion cuisine from celebrity chef Bobby Flay, whose specialties include mango and spice-crusted tuna, and salmon tartare in purple maize tortillas. And don't forget the fruit margaritas, which leave you with a warm glow inside.

🚰 C8–D8 ⊠ Caesars Palace, 3570 Las Vegas Boulevard South ☎ 877/346-4642 🕔 Mon–Fri 11–3.30, 5–11, Sat–Sun 10.30–3, 5–11 🚌 Deuce

MICHAEL MINA $$$

www.bellagiolasvegas.net

Enjoy seafood favorites that chef Michael Mina has made famous with his daring approach, using unexpected flavors and textures

DINING WITH A VIEW

There are some wonderful spots in Vegas where you can savor great views while you eat, but one of the best is the Top of the World restaurant (▷ 149). On the 106th floor of the Stratosphere Tower, it makes one revolution in 60 minutes, during which you can see The Strip, the mountains, the valleys and beyond. Also try Mona Ami Gabi (▷ above).

blended with Mediterranean and Californian ingredients. Sleek, yet casual, this is the perfect place to try Mina's signature dishes.

🚰 C9–D9 ⊠ Bellagio, 3600 Las Vegas Boulevard South ☎ 702/693-7223 🕔 Thu–Tue 5.30–10pm 🚌 Deuce

MON AMI GABI $$

www.monamigabi.com

Fine French fare is served in the atrium (with an open sunroof) or on the patio. Tables are set beneath sparkling lights, from where you get a great view of the Bellagio's fountain show.

🚰 D9 ⊠ Paris Las Vegas, 3655 Las Vegas Boulevard South ☎ 702/944-4224 🕔 Sun–Thu 11.30–3, 4–11, Fri–Sat 11.30–3, 4–12 🚌 Deuce

NERO'S $$$

www.caesarspalace.com

Maine lobster, swordfish and grilled ahi feature on the menu of this popular restaurant, along with hearty steaks. The beef is top-quality, prime Black Angus, and other specialties include Colorado lamb chops.

🚰 C8–D8 ⊠ Caesars Palace, 3570 Las Vegas Boulevard South ☎ 702/731-7110 🕔 Daily 5–11pm 🚌 Deuce

NOBHILL TAVERN $$$

www.mgmgrand.com

A taste of San Francisco is brought to Las Vegas by celebrity chef Michael Mina. Try any of the five kinds of whipped potatoes, Tasmanian ocean trout, lobster pot pie or beef rib eye with seared foie gras.

🚰 D10 ⊠ MGM Grand, 3799 Las Vegas Boulevard South ☎ 702/891-7337 🕔 Sun–Thu 5.30–10pm, Fri–Sat 5.30–10.30pm 🚌 Deuce

NOODLE SHOP $

www.mandalaybay.com

The food here really hits the spot when you need sustenance at any time of day. It offers over 20 kinds of noodle-and-rice dishes, served hot and at lightning speed, plus barbecued meat dishes.

🔢 D11 ✉ Mandalay Bay, 3950 Las Vegas Boulevard South ☎ 702/632-6071 🕐 Sun–Thu 11–11, Fri–Sat 11am–1am 🚍 Deuce

PAMPAS BRAZILIAN GRILLE $$

www.pampasusa.com

Come enjoy the true taste of Brazil. Sizzling skewers of the finest meats are bought to your table in an endless parade while you feast on mountains of fresh produce and salads at the buffet.

🔢 D9 ✉ Miracle Mile, 3663 Las Vegas Boulevard South ☎ 702/737-4748 🕐 Daily 8am–10.30pm 🚍 Deuce

PARADISE GARDEN BUFFET $$

www.flamingolasvegas.com

Enjoy the view of cascading waterfalls and playful antics of the Flamingo's wildlife while you dine on crab, shrimp, prime rib, salads and everything else in between. Leave room for one of the delicious desserts.

🔢 D9 ✉ Flamingo, 3555 Las Vegas Boulevard South ☎ 702/733-3111 🕐 Daily 7am–10pm 🚍 Deuce

PICASSO $$$

www.bellagiolasvegas.com

This is among the best restaurants in Vegas, with refined cuisine reflecting places where the artist lived (south of France and Spain). The Picasso paintings on the walls are authentic.

JUST DESSERTS

If it's dessert you're after, then pay a visit to Lenôtre in Le Boulevard at Paris Las Vegas (▷ 49) for a mouthwatering assortment of French pastries, éclairs and cookies that can be enjoyed in a café-style atmosphere. At the Venetian (▷ 58–59), Tintoretto's Bakery also has luscious homemade pastries and cookies.

🔢 C9–D9 ✉ Bellagio, 3600 Las Vegas Boulevard South ☎ 702/693-7223 🕐 Wed–Mon 6–9.30pm 🚍 Deuce

PIERO'S $$$

www.pieroscuisine.com

Sublime Italian cuisine—frequently voted the best in Vegas—is served at Piero's, one of the city's most established restaurants. Former patrons include George Bush Sr., Arnold Schwarzenegger and Keith Richards, and the rich and famous are still drawn to its bustling but hassle-free ambience. Osso bucco, one of Piero's signature dishes, melts in the mouth, and the fish and seafood are also excellent. Garbage Caesar is tastier than it sounds: Caesar salad with palm hearts and shrimps.

🔢 E7 ✉ 335 Convention Center Drive ☎ 702/369-2305 🕐 Daily 5.30–10pm 🚍 213

POSTRIO $$

www.venetian.com

Enjoy celebrity chef Wolfgang Puck's American dishes in the elegant dining room or in the more casual café looking out on St. Mark's Square.

🔢 D8 ✉ The Venetian, 3355 Las Vegas Boulevard South ☎ 702/369-0558 🕐 Sun–Thu 11–10, Fri–Sat 11–10.30 🚍 Deuce

EAT

RA $$

www.rasushi.com

An upbeat, casual mood creates the perfect setting to enjoy fresh sushi, Japanese-fusion cuisine and signature dishes so good that you can't wait to return. Bright wall hangings and globe lighting accent the interior.

🔢 D7 ⊠ Fashion Show Mall, 3200 Las Vegas Boulevard South ☎ 702/696-0008 🕙 Daily 11am–midnight 🚌 Deuce

RED SQUARE $$

www.mandalaybay.com

Wash latkes and blinis down with vodka, or choose US and French dishes in this Russian-theme restaurant, where the headless statue of Lenin, the red-velvet drapes and the fake Communist propaganda give the game away.

🔢 D11 ⊠ Mandalay Bay, 3950 Las Vegas Boulevard South ☎ 702/632-7407 🕙 Daily 5–10.30pm 🚌 Deuce

SECOND STREET GRILL $$

www.fremontcasino.com

Step back in time at this hidden gem and sample good Pacific Rim and contemporary cuisine at affordable prices. Soft lighting and rich woods encourage you to relax in the oversized chairs.

🔢 G3 ⊠ Fremont Casino, 200 Fremont Street ☎ 702/385-3232 🕙 Sun–Mon, Thu 5–10pm, Fri–Sat 5–11pm 🚌 108, Deuce

THE STEAK HOUSE $$

www.circuscircus.com

This old-timer is popular for its succulent prime ribs and tasty grilled steaks, all at low prices. There's seafood, lobster, chicken and lamb as well.

🔢 E6 ⊠ Circus Circus, 2880 Las Vegas Boulevard South ☎ 702/734-0410 🕙 Sun–Fri 5–10pm, Sat 5–11pm 🚌 Deuce

STRIP HOUSE $$$

www.striphouse.com

Excellent traditional American cuisine is served in this darkly lit and intimate restaurant, whose walls are lined with 1920s black-and-white portraits of magazine pin-up models. Seafood dishes include Maine lobster linguine, lump crab cake, pan-seared red salmon and New England sea

Dining at the Stratosphere Tower's Top of the World revolving restaurant

scallop. The steaks are for serious carnivores, up to a massive 20oz (565g) New York Strip T-bone.

⊞ D9 ⊠ Planet Hollywood, 3667 Las Vegas Boulevard South ☎ 702/737-5200 🕘 Sun–Thu 5–11pm, Fri–Sat 5–11.30pm 🚍 Deuce

TOP OF THE WORLD $$$

www.topoftheworldlv.com

Master chefs Rick Giffen and Claude Gaty have achieved the seemingly impossible at this stylish revolving restaurant: to upstage the best view in the city with some of the best food in Vegas. Parisian Gaty mixes traditional French cuisine with flavor-packed Asian twists, such as crab cakes with ginger slaw and roast miso black cod to die for. The tasting menu is a gastronomic roller coaster to rival the white-knuckle lunacy going on up above. It's worth every cent.

⊞ E5–F5 ⊠ Stratosphere Tower, 2000 Las Vegas Boulevard South ☎ 702/380-7711 🕘 Daily 11–11 🚍 Deuce

TOTO'S $

This family-run restaurant serves enormous helpings of great Mexican food. It's very popular with locals who appreciate the good value.

⊞ H10 ⊠ 2055 East Tropicana Avenue ☎ 702/ 895-7923 🕘 Daily 11–10 🚍 201

TRIPLE GEORGE GRILL $$–$$$

www.triplegeorgegrill.com

A popular joint, this sophisticated grill offers reliable quality steaks, fine seafood dishes, yummy desserts and a remarkable service. Portions are big so you may want to share a dish.

⊞ G3 ⊠ 201 North Third Street ☎ 702/384-2761 🕘 Mon 11–4, Tue–Fri 11–10, Sat 4–10pm 🚍 108, Deuce

VALENTINO $$$

www.venetian.com

Linger over superb modern Italian cuisine in a remarkable setting at this top-class restaurant, owned by unforgettable Piero Selvaggio.

⊞ D8 ⊠ The Venetian, 3355 Las Vegas Boulevard South ☎ 702/414-3000 🕘 Daily 5.30–10pm 🚍 Deuce

VERANDAH HIGH TEA $$

www.fourseasons.com/lasvegas

It's quite a surprise to find that great British institution, afternoon tea, in the middle of Vegas. Have sandwiches, scones with cream and jam, and French pastries, plus a selection of fine teas. Piano music completes the elegant scene. Reservations are required.

⊞ D11 ⊠ Four Seasons, 3960 Las Vegas Boulevard South ☎ 702/632-5000 🕘 Mon–Fri 6.30am–10pm, Sat–Sun 7am–10pm 🚍 Deuce

VILLAGE SEAFOOD $$

www.riolasvegas.com

Fish, fish and more fish—in fact, nothing but seafood—is served at this buffet. There's plenty of choice, with dishes prepared in every way you could imagine.

⊞ B8 ⊠ Rio, 3700 West Flamingo Road ☎ 702/777-7777 🕘 Mon–Fri 4–10pm, Sat–Sun 3.30–10.30pm 🚍 202

EAT

Sleep

Ranging from luxurious and modern upmarket hotels to simple budget hotels, Las Vegas has accommodations to suit everyone. In this section establishments are listed alphabetically.

SLEEP

Introduction

Las Vegas is one of the few cities where you can eat, drink, shop and be entertained without even needing to leave your hotel.

Hotels

For a truly unique experience, stay in one of the theme casino hotels on and around The Strip. These are like no others in the world and give you the added benefit of being right in the heart of the action. An increasing number of smaller, more exclusive hotels are popping up that offer an alternative for those who want time out away from the neon jungle. The north end of The Strip has seen better days in places. Some bastions of the "Golden Era" remain and have undergone extensive renovations, while others are being torn down to make way for dazzling new resorts. If you want a taste of nostalgia, choose a hotel in historic Downtown, a favorite with millions of visitors.

Motels

Las Vegas boasts dozens of motels near The Strip and downtown. Rates can be rock-bottom and their rooms are normally the last to get booked up, making them a good bet for finding a last-minute room. Motels don't have casinos, which also means they don't have large crowds. Don't expect much more than standard motel lodgings.

GETTING THE BEST DEAL

For the best deal start looking well in advance: In Las Vegas it really does pay to shop around. Set a budget, know where you would like to stay and in what type of accommodations. Generally, prices are lower during the week but room rates fluctuate according to demand—they can change from day to day. Check to see if the city is staging a major convention before deciding when to go, as accommodations will be in demand, making prices higher. If you do your homework first, it's possible to get a luxury hotel room at a budget price.

From top: Circus Circus, one of the oldest hotels on The Strip; Motel 8 Las Vegas sign; the exquisite lobby of Paris Las Vegas

SLEEP

Directory

South Strip

Budget
Doubletree Club
Mid-Range
Emerald Suites—Las Vegas Blvd
Excalibur
Hooters
Luxor
MGM Grand
Monte Carlo
New York-New York
Luxury
Four Seasons Las Vegas
Mandalay Bay

Central Strip

Budget
Bally's Las Vegas
Fairfield Inn Las Vegas Airport
Flamingo Las Vegas
Terrible's

Mid-Range
Alexis Park
Palazzo
Palms Resort
Rio All-Suite Hotel
Treasure Island
The Venetian
Luxury
ARIA
Bellagio
Caesars Palace
The Cosmopolitan of Las Vegas
Platinum Hotel and Spa
Renaissance Las Vegas

North Strip

Budget
Circus Circus
Royal Resort
Sin City Hostel
Somerset House

Mid-Range
Courtyard by Marriott
Howard Johnson—Las Vegas Strip
Las Vegas Hilton
Riviera
Luxury
Wynn Las Vegas

Downtown

Budget
Main Street Station

Further Afield

Budget
Hawthorn Suites

Sleeping A-Z

PRICES

Prices are approximate and based on a double room for one night.

$$$	over $200
$$	$120–$200
$	under $120

ALEXIS PARK $$

www.alexispark.com
If you prefer to stay off The Strip, this small hotel, with 495 rooms, has some great two-level suites for a really good price. It's also fairly quiet here. Facilities include a spa and three pools.

➕ E9 ✉ 375 East Harmon Avenue ☎ 702/796-3300 🚌 108

ARIA $$$

www.arialasvegas.com
ARIA is the flagship hotel of the stunning new CityCenter complex (▷ 22–23). The rooms and suites have floor-to-ceiling windows to match the glass-walled tower's smooth lines. Top-of-the-range gourmet dining, elite nightclubs and entertainment headed by Cirque de Soleil's latest production, Viva ELVIS (▷ 74), will make it hard for you to leave the premises.
➕ C10 ✉ 3730 Las Vegas Boulevard South ☎ 702/590-7757 🚌 Deuce

BALLY'S LAS VEGAS $

www.ballyslasvegas.com

Bally's is less oriented toward a lively young crowd or families. The 2,814 rooms and 265 suites are sumptuous, with grand sitting rooms and opulent bathrooms. There are floodlit tennis courts.

➕ D9 ✉ 3645 Las Vegas Boulevard South ☎ 702/739-4111 🚌 Deuce

BELLAGIO (▷ 16) $$$

www.bellagio.com

This is one of the most beautiful hotels in Vegas, built in the style of a huge Mediterranean villa with lovely gardens. The 3,930-plus rooms and suites are large and classy, decorated in natural hues.

➕ C9–D9 ✉ 3600 Las Vegas Boulevard South ☎ 702/693-7111 🚌 Deuce

CAESARS PALACE (▷ 18) $$$

www.caesarspalace.com

Ancient Rome prevails through classical temples, marble columns and every possible excess you can imagine. All 3,300 rooms and suites are luxurious, but even more so in the Palace, the Forum and Augustus tower, which have huge whirlpool tubs in the bathrooms, and extras such as an LCD TV screen in the bathroom mirror.

➕ C8–D8 ✉ 3570 Las Vegas Boulevard South ☎ 702/731-7110 🚌 Deuce

CIRCUS CIRCUS (▷ 20) $

www.circuscircus.com

Although it is one of the oldest hotels on The Strip, Circus Circus still provides one of the best value-for-money options if you have kids with you. It has 3,770 rooms and 130 suites.

➕ E6 ✉ 2880 Las Vegas Boulevard South ☎ 702/734-0410 🚌 Deuce

THE COSMOPOLITAN OF LAS VEGAS $$$

www.cosmopolitanlasvegas.com

Opened at the end of 2010, the sheer-sided tower of The Cosmopolitan, next door to the

The Flamingo is a good choice if you want to be close to the action

happening CityCenter (▷ 22–23), offers nearly 3,000 rooms, studios and suites, some with balconies (a rarity on The Strip) and all with a kitchenette. With a focus on hip nightlife, its central showpiece is an amazing multistory dripping chandelier, which drapes around several bars and lounges, dazzling its trendy guests with literal sparkle.

➕ D9 ✉ 3708 Las Vegas Boulevard South ☎ 702/698-7000 🚍 Deuce

COURTYARD BY MARRIOTT $$

www.courtyard.com/LASCH
Part of the well-known chain, this hotel provides 149 nicer-than-the-average motel rooms (including 12 suites). It's located opposite the Las Vegas Convention Center.

➕ F7 ✉ 3275 Paradise Road ☎ 702/791-3600 🚍 108

DOUBLETREE CLUB $

www.lasvegasairportclub.doubletree.com
This plain concrete block is just 10 minutes from the airport, but is surprisingly quiet, and handy for late arrivals or early departures. The excellent value big rooms have all mod-cons and free internet. There are regular free shuttles to the airport and to The Strip.

➕ E12 ✉ 7250 Pollock Drive ☎ 702/948-4000

EMERALD SUITES – LAS VEGAS BLVD $$

www.emeraldsuites.com
On The Strip, south of Mandalay Bay Resort, this non-gaming establishment features more than 250 suites, with both one and two bedrooms, each tastefully decorated and equipped with a fully fitted kitchen. Guests have

the use of a lagoon-style pool nestled in pleasant landscaping.

➕ Off map ✉ 9145 Las Vegas Boulevard South ☎ 702/948-9999 🚍 117

EXCALIBUR (▷ 28) $$

www.excalibur.com
Kids love this medieval castle, with its moat and drawbridge. Parents might find it all just a little tacky, but it's probably the best deal on The Strip, and has 3,991 rooms.

➕ D10 ✉ 3850 Las Vegas Boulevard South ☎ 702/597-7777 🚍 Deuce

FAIRFIELD INN LAS VEGAS AIRPORT $

www.fairfieldinn.com
Two blocks east of The Strip, this pristine, small—in Vegas terms—hotel has a contemporary design. The 142 rooms and suites have a living area and are decorated in cheerful hues. Start your day with the "Early Eats" complimentary breakfast. There's an outdoor swimming pool and fitness center.

➕ F8 ✉ 3850 Paradise Road ☎ 702/895-9810 🚍 108

FLAMINGO LAS VEGAS $

www.flamingolasvegas.com
Bugsy Siegel's original 1946 Flamingo was rebuilt by the Hilton

SLEEP

group in 1993. The modern hotel has 3,565 units in all; the deluxe king rooms are spacious. The Flamingo also has one of the best pool areas on The Strip, and it's close to the action.

➕ D9 ✉ 3555 Las Vegas Boulevard South ☎ 702/733-3111 🚌 Deuce

FOUR SEASONS LAS VEGAS $$$

www.fourseasons.com

This hotel takes up the top five levels of the Mandalay Bay (▷ 157), but retains its own tranquil identity. The 424 rooms and suites are elegantly decorated in peach, aqua and gold, and all the Mandalay Bay facilities are available to guests.

➕ D11 ✉ 3960 Las Vegas Boulevard South ☎ 702/632-5000 🚌 Deuce

HAWTHORN SUITES $

www.hawthorn.com

Hawthorn Suites is an appealing alternative if you prefer some distance between you and The Strip, but not too far off the beaten track. It's a good choice for families; the suites are plain but have kitchens and a balcony, and lots of extras. There are 70 rooms, an indoor pool and fitness center.

➕ Off map ✉ 910 Boulder Highway, Henderson ☎ 702/568-7800 🚌 217

HOOTERS $$

www.hooterscasinohotel.com

It's all surfboards and palm trees at this remodeled casino-hotel. Floridian-style bedrooms, some in a bungalow building separate from the main towers, are bright and sunny. Hooters is more intimate than some of the Vegas giants and has a fun atmosphere and friendly staff. There are over 650 rooms.

➕ D10 ✉ 115 East Tropicana ☎ 702/739-9000 🚌 201

HOWARD JOHNSON – LAS VEGAS STRIP $$

www.howardjohnsonlasvegasstrip.com

This low-rise motel is in a good location at the north end of The Strip. Some of the 100 rooms have a whirlpool bath.

➕ F4 ✉ 1401 Las Vegas Boulevard South ☎ 702/388-0301 🚌 Deuce

LAS VEGAS HILTON $$

www.lvhilton.com

This old-timer still offers fine accommodations in its 3,000 guest rooms, with individual opulent style. Elvis staged his comeback here in 1969 to 1977 (note the statue at the entrance), and the hotel was used in the Bond film *Diamonds are Forever*.

➕ F7 ✉ 3000 Paradise Road ☎ 702/732-5111 🚌 108

LUXOR (▷ 38) $$

www.luxor.com

The 4,400-room Luxor may have moved away from its original Egyptian theme but you still enter beneath a huge sphinx and are transported to your room via an elevator that travels up the slope of the pyramid.

🔲 C11 D11 ✉ 3900 Las Vegas Boulevard South ☎ 702/262-4000 🚌 Deuce

MAIN STREET STATION $

www.mainstreetcasino.com

This characterful hotel has a Victorian theme, with genuine antiques, chandeliers, flickering gas lamps, iron railings and stained-glass windows. It has 406 bright rooms.

🔲 G2 ✉ 200 North Main Street ☎ 702/387-1896 🚌 108, Deuce

MANDALAY BAY $$$

www.mandalaybay.com

There is masses of big-city style at the Mandalay Bay. It's the only hotel in Las Vegas with a beach and a gigantic wave pool. There are 3,200-plus rooms and suites; even the standard rooms are huge, and all are light and airy.

🔲 D11 ✉ 3950 Las Vegas Boulevard South ☎ 702/632-7777 🚌 Deuce

MGM GRAND $$

www.mgmgrand.com

This is pure Hollywood, with figures of famous stars dotted around the lobby and huge stills from classic movies on the walls. The 5,000-plus rooms offer a range of options, from the small Emerald Tower rooms to large spacious suites.

🔲 D10 ✉ 3799 Las Vegas Boulevard South ☎ 702/891-1111 🚌 Deuce

MONTE CARLO $$

www.montecarlo.com

A popular choice with golfers (it has a full-time golf concierge), the Monte Carlo has around 3,000 attractive rooms and suites.

🔲 D10 ✉ 3770 Las Vegas Boulevard South ☎ 702/730-7777 🚌 Deuce

NEW YORK-NEW YORK (▷ 46) $$

www.nynyhotelcasino.com

This huge mock-up of the New York skyline is an experience to stay at. The 2,023 rooms are in a sophisticated '40s-style, decorated in earth tones and pastels. Light sleepers should request a room away from the Roller Coaster that thunders around the outside.

🔲 D10 ✉ 3790 Las Vegas Boulevard South ☎ 702/740-6969 🚌 Deuce

PALAZZO $$

www.palazzo.com

Palazzo is a magnificent all-suite sister hotel to The Venetian (▷ 58–59), with similar Italian-style decor. The superb suites have fantastic views from higher floors.

🔲 D8 ✉ 3325 Las Vegas Boulevard South ☎ 702/607-7777 🚌 Deuce

HOTEL TIPPING

As in any US city, it is customary to offer a gratuity to hotel employees for prompt and courteous service. Las Vegas has a huge amount of different staff who provide such services, and who gets what can be confusing. The amount is at the customer's discretion but here are some general guidelines: bell captains and bellhops $1–$2 per bag; hotel maids $2 per day upon departure; valets $2; use of concierge or VIP services $5; waiters and waitresses 15 to 20 percent of the bill.

PALMS RESORT $$

www.palms.com

As the name suggests, expect plenty of tropical foliage at this towering hotel. The Palms' hot-spot reputation is due mainly to the clientele attracted to its nighttime haunts, such as the Ghostbar (▷ 130). The 700 bedrooms are luxurious, with huge bathrooms.

✚ A9 ⊠ 4321 West Flamingo Road ☎ 702/942-7777 🚌 202

PLATINUM HOTEL AND SPA $$$

www.theplatinumhotel.com

Opened July 2006, this non-gaming, smoke-free retreat is in lavish contemporary style. The spacious 255 one- and two-bedroom suites have a kitchen, whirlpool tub and a balcony overlooking The Strip or mountains. Make use of the soothing spa or indoor and outdoor pools.

✚ E9 ⊠ 211 East Flamingo Road ☎ 702/365-5000 🚌 202

RENAISSANCE LAS VEGAS $$$

www.renaissancelasvegas.com

For a retreat from the Vegas clamor and commotion, the Renaissance has cool and confident style without a slot machine in sight. The 578 rooms and suites are richly decorated and have a calming feel. There's also a swimming pool, whirlpool and fitness center.

✚ F7 ⊠ 3400 Paradise Road ☎ 702/784-5700 🚌 108

RIO ALL-SUITE HOTEL $$

www.riolasvegas.com

This is a lively hotel in an off-Strip location, with great nightlife and two excellent buffets among its dining options. It has 2,548 huge and plush suites, with superb views from the floor-to-ceiling windows.

✚ B8 ⊠ 3700 West Flamingo Road ☎ 702/777-7777 🚌 202

RIVIERA $$

www.rivierahotel.com

The Riviera is a good choice at the quieter north end of The Strip, with stylishly muted rooms and suites. It is one of the more long-standing hotel-casinos, with a reputation for raunchy entertainment.

✚ E6–E7 ⊠ 2901 Las Vegas Boulevard South ☎ 702/734-5110 🚌 Deuce

ROYAL RESORT $

www.royalhotelvegas.com

The quiet non-casino Royal Resort is just off The Strip, between the Fashion Show Mall and Circus

The lobby of the Palazzo (▷ 157)

Circus, and offers good value for money. It has small but comfortable rooms; those at the front have a private balcony. Other amenities include a restaurant (breakfasts at extra cost), bar, outdoor pool and gym.

➕ E7 ✉ 199 Convention Center Drive
☎ 702/735-6117 🚌 Deuce

SIN CITY HOSTEL $

www.sincityhostel.com
This is the only hostel on The Strip, with dorms and semi-private rooms. There are no frills, but it's clean, with friendly staff and a fun atmosphere, and includes a free continental breakfast.

➕ F4 ✉ 1208 Las Vegas Boulevard South, Downtown (north of Stratosphere Tower)
☎ 702/868-0222 🚌 Deuce

SOMERSET HOUSE $

Handy for the Convention Center, and one block off The Strip, this good-value motel has 104 rooms and minisuites.

➕ E7 ✉ 294 Convention Center Drive
☎ 702/735-4411 🚌 108, Deuce

TERRIBLE'S $

www.herbstgaming.com
Don't be fooled by the name, as this small hotel near The Strip is anything but terrible. The 374 pleasant rooms are basic, but clean, at very agreeable rates.

➕ F9 ✉ 4100 Paradise Road
☎ 702/733-7000 🚌 108

TREASURE ISLAND (TI) $$

www.treasureisland.com
This hotel has left behind its Pirates of the Caribbean swashbuckling image for a more sophisticated adult take on the high seas. The 3,000 rooms and

suites, decorated in French Regency style, have floor-to-ceiling windows—Strip side, there's no better view of the Sirens of TI pirate battle (▷ 73).

➕ D8 ✉ 3300 Las Vegas Boulevard South
☎ 702/894-7111 🚌 Deuce

THE VENETIAN (▷ 58) $$

www.venetian.com
Famous for its canals and replica of St. Mark's Square, The Venetian has 4,027 rooms (actually they are all suites). The decor varies, although all have marble bathrooms and fine furnishings. There are also excellent dining and shopping opportunities.

➕ D8 ✉ 3355 Las Vegas Boulevard South
☎ 702/414-1000 🚌 Deuce

WYNN LAS VEGAS (▷ 62) $$$

www.wynnlasvegas.com
Steve Wynn's latest incredible hotel-casino is one of the world's most expensive hotels, and occupies 60 floors. The 2,700-plus rooms are huge, very stylish, and are equipped with every luxury. There is a private lake, man-made mountain and 18-hole golf course.

➕ D7–E7 ✉ 3131 Las Vegas Boulevard South ☎ 702/770-7000 Center 🚌 Deuce

Need to Know

This section takes you through all the practical aspects of your trip to make it run more smoothly and to give you confidence before you go and while you are there.

Planning Ahead

WHEN TO GO

With so many of its attractions under cover and not dependent on weather conditions, there's no off-season to speak of in Las Vegas. Avoid high summer if you don't like excessively hot weather, unless you plan to stay indoors.

TIME

Vegas is on Pacific Standard Time (GMT –8), advanced one hour between early April and early October.

TEMPERATURE

	JAN	FEB	MAR	APR	MAY	JUN	JUL	AUG	SEP	OCT	NOV	DEC
°F	56°F	62°F	68°F	78°F	88°F	98°F	104°F	102°F	94°F	81°F	66°F	57°F
°C	13°C	17°C	20°C	25°C	31°C	36°C	40°C	39°C	34°C	27°C	19°C	14°C

Summer (June to September) can be incredibly hot and oppressive, with daytime temperatures sometimes soaring as high as 120°F (49°C).

Spring and autumn are much more comfortable, with average temperatures usually reaching 70°F (21°C).

Winter (December to February) sees average temperatures above 50°F (10°C). There can be the odd chillier day when you will need a jacket, and sometimes it can drop below freezing at night.

WHAT'S ON

January *Laughlin Desert Challenge:* Top drivers compete in an off-road motor race over rough terrain.

March *NASCAR Nextel Cup Race* (early Mar): A major event on the racing calendar, held at the Las Vegas Motor Speedway.
St. Patrick's Day Parade (Mar 17): A parade of floats downtown kicks off other entertainment; Celtic bands, storytellers and dancers.

May *Billboard Music Awards:* Music celebrities gather at the MGM Grand Garden Arena to honor the world's best music.

May/July *World Series of Poker:* The world's best poker players compete for supremacy at Harrah's Rio.

June *CineVegas International Film Festival* (early Jun): Film debuts from studios, with celebrities attending the huge parties.

September *International Mariachi Festival:* A popular Mexican festival that takes place at the Paris Theatre, in the Paris Las Vegas hotel.

October/November *Professional Bull Riders World Finals:* Two weekends at Mandalay Bay and Thomas & Mack Center.

November *Comedy Festival:* A festival in multiple venues throughout Caesars Palace, with dozens of performers and special events.

December *National Finals Rodeo* (early Dec): During the 10-day finals, cowboys compete and Las Vegas goes country-mad, dressing up, line-dancing and barbecuing.
New Year's Eve Celebrations: A party held at Fremont Street.

First Friday A huge arts and entertainment party takes place on the first Friday of each month in the Arts District downtown (✉ 702/384-0092; www. firstfriday-lasvegas.org ⏱ 6–10pm).

LAS VEGAS ONLINE

www.visitlasvegas.com
The official website of Las Vegas Convention and Visitors Authority offers well-presented information on everything you need to know when planning your trip to Las Vegas.

www.lasvegas.com
For articles on local news, listings, events and other sources of information, try this useful site run by the respected *Review Journal*, Nevada's largest newspaper.

www.vegas.com
This informative site geared to visitors has honest reviews of restaurants, bars, shows and nightlife, and gives access to hotel and show reservations.

www.lasvegasgolf.com
To help you plan a golfing holiday in Las Vegas, this site has detailed reviews on all the courses open in Vegas and other US cities.

www.vegasexperience.com
This lively site is dedicated to the Fremont Street Experience. See what's going on at any time of the year and look for places to stay and eat.

www.gayvegas.com
The most complete site for gay locals and visitors to Las Vegas. It keeps up with the latest information on clubs, bars, restaurants and organizations, plus lots more.

www.nightonthetown.com
For one of the most comprehensive and easy-to-use guides to eating out, entertainment and hotels, check out this site. The restaurants are listed by cuisine type and location.

www.cheapovegas.com
Geared to the visitor who wants to do Vegas on a budget, this fun guide provides comprehensive reviews and unbiased opinions with a humorous slant.

PRIME TRAVEL SITES

www.rtcsnv.com/transit/
Official site for the Regional Transportation Commission of Southern Nevada (RTC), the company responsible for the Las Vegas bus system. Use the transit system map, routes and schedule pages to discover exactly how to get from A to B.

www.fodors.com
A complete travel-planning site where you can research prices and weather; book air tickets, cars and rooms; pose questions (and get answers) to fellow visitors; and find links to other sites.

INTERNET ACCESS

Most hotels in Las Vegas have business centers and offer internet access to their guests, but you have to be aware that most hotels charge for internet access (around $10–$20 per day), and for WiFi connection when using your own laptop. It is possible to find free access in some hotels, but you will need to enquire on arrival or look online. Try: http://govegas.about.com For cafés try: www.cybercafes.com, which is an up-to-date search engine enabling you to locate internet cafés all over the world.

NEED TO KNOW

Getting There

ENTRY REQUIREMENTS

Visitors to the US must show a full passport, valid for at least six months. You must complete an Electronic System of Travel Authorization (ESTA™) before traveling to the USA. ESTA™ is a web-based system and can only be accessed online. For more information, and to complete the form visit https://esta.cbp.dhs.gov. Most UK citizens and visitors from other countries belonging to the Visa Waiver Program can enter without a visa, but must have a return or onward ticket. Allow extra time for security checks. Regulations can change, so check before you travel with the US Embassy (☎ 020 7499 9000; www.usembassy.org.uk).

AIRPORT FACTS

● McCarran airport has two well-organized terminals with many shops, restaurants and snack bars.
● It has recently undergone a $500 million expansion, with a new international terminal opening in 2012.
● 47 million passengers per year pass through the airport.
● It is among the 15 busiest airports in the world.
● It is one of a few airports where you can play the slot machines while waiting for your luggage, or visit the 24-hour fitness center.

AIRPORT

McCarran International Airport (LAS) is served by direct flights from cities right across North America, and there are intercontinental flights from London, Frankfurt and Tokyo. It is worth checking for special deals from airline and flight brokers, in newspapers and on the internet.

FROM MCCARRAN INTERNATIONAL AIRPORT

The McCarran airport terminal (tel 702/261-5211; www.mccarran.com) is 4 miles (6km) southeast of The Strip, at 5757 Wayne Newton Boulevard. There is a ground Transportation Center near baggage claim for shuttles and for renting cars and limousines, and information desks can be found throughout the airport.

Several companies run airport shuttle buses every 10 or 15 minutes from just outside the baggage claim area—leave through door exits 7–13. They all cost roughly the same (about $6.50 to The Strip and $8 to Downtown) and normally operate 24 hours. Most stop at all the major hotels and motels. For advance reservations for shuttles, tel 702/558-9155. Check first, as your resort hotel might offer an airport shuttle. Less expensive are the CAT buses (about $1.25 one way) that operate from outside the airport terminal: No. 108 will take you to the Las Vegas Hilton, from where you can transfer to the Deuce (▷ 166), which stops close to most hotels along The Strip; and No. 109 goes to the Downtown Transportation Center.

Taxis are easily available outside baggage claim, and cost $8.20 to The Strip, or $20 to Downtown hotels (depends on traffic and destination). Stretch limos line up outside the airport waiting to take you to your destination; if you are tempted, try to share as they can be costly ($55 up to $125 per hour, depending on the size). Try Ambassador Limousines (tel 702/362-6200) or Las Vegas Limousines (tel 702/736-1419). For car rentals, all major car rental companies are represented inside the airport's arrival hall (▷ panel). There are buses and shuttles available to take you to the rental company you are using. It is better to reserve a car in advance.

ARRIVING BY BUS

Greyhound/Trailways (www.greyhound.com) operates services to Las Vegas from most cities and towns in California and Nevada. Tickets can be purchased just prior to departure. This is a convenient and inexpensive way to travel, although not the most comfortable. All Greyhound buses arrive at Downtown's bus terminal at 200 South Main Street (tel 702/383-9792).

ARRIVING BY CAR

Interstate 15 from Los Angeles to Vegas takes you through some of the most breathtaking scenery of the Mojave Desert. The journey takes 4–5 hours depending on road, weather and traffic conditions (delays are often caused by construction work). Carry plenty of water and a spare tire, and keep an eye on your fuel level.

ARRIVING BY RAIL

Amtrak, the national train company, does not offer a direct service to Las Vegas. You can connect to the city by bus from other rail destinations in California and Arizona. Amtrak has talked of restoring the line from Los Angeles to Las Vegas, but at the time of writing nothing had materialized. Contact Amtrak (tel 800/872-7245; www.amtrak.com) for the latest details.

CAR RENTAL

Hotel information desks can advise about renting a car. Rental companies will deliver to hotels and pick up at the end of the rental period.

Avis	702/531-1500
Budget	702/736-1212
Enterprise	702/795-8842
Hertz	702/262-7700
National	702/263-8411
Thrifty	702/896-7600

There is a centralized rent-a-car center at McCarran Airport serviced by all the major rental companies. All customers will be transported to their vehicles by dedicated free shuttles. For information, call 702/261-6001.

CUSTOMS

● Visitors from outside the US, aged 21 or over, may import duty-free: 200 cigarettes, or 50 non-Cuban cigars, or 2kg of tobacco; 1 liter of alcohol; and gifts up to $100 in value.
● Imports of wildlife souvenirs sourced from rare or endangered species may be illegal or require a special permit. Check your home country's customs rules.
● Restricted import items include meat, seeds, plants and fruit.
● Some medication bought over the counter abroad may be prescription-only in the US and could be confiscated. Bring a doctor's certificate for essential medication.

Getting Around

VISITORS WITH DISABILITIES

If you are a wheelchair-user, on arrival at the airport you will find shuttle buses with wheelchair lifts to get you into the city. You will also find easy access to most restaurants, showrooms and lounges. All the hotel casinos have accessible slot machines, and many provide access to table games. Assisted listening devices are widely available. If you plan to rent a car, you can request a free 90-day disabled parking permit, which can be used throughout Vegas; contact the City of Las Vegas Parking Permit Office (☎ 702/229-6431).
Las Vegas Convention and Visitors Authority ADA coordinator
☎ 702/892-0711

WALKING

The Strip is 3.5 miles (5.5km) long, and it's a taxing walk in the heat. Wear comfortable shoes, sunglasses and sunscreen. Even if you use The Strip's transportation, you will still have to walk considerable distances to and from hotels and attractions. Overhead walkways connect several places along The Strip. Make a note of the cross streets that punctuate The Strip to help get your bearings; some are named after the hotels along them.

Most of what you will want to see and do in Las Vegas is found along Las Vegas Boulevard, which is well served by buses. The boulevard is divided into two parts: Downtown, between Charleston Boulevard and Washington Avenue; and The Strip, comprising several long blocks—Sahara, Spring Mountain, Flamingo, Tropicana and Russell. In 2004 the first leg of a multimillion dollar monorail was launched, providing a welcome addition to the options for getting up and down The Strip.

BUSES

CAT, Citizens Area Transit, run by the RTC (Regional Transportation Commission of Southern Nevada (▷ 163), tel 702/228-7433), runs 51 bus routes throughout the entire system, of which 24 operate 24 hours a day. The Downtown Transportation Center (DTC) at Casino Center Boulevard and South Strip Transfer Terminal (SSTT) at Gillespie Street are major transfer points. The Deuce provides transportation along The Strip from the DTC to the SSTT, with many stops along the way, and runs about every 10 minutes (during peak times), 24 hours a day. This double-decker bus, launched in 2005, accommodates 97 people. The fare is $2 one-way or $7 for a day pass, which you can purchase on the bus or from vending machines (you need to have the exact fare because drivers can't give change). You can get a transfer from the driver for off-Strip destinations, so you don't have to pay again. Off-strip buses otherwise cost $1.25 one-way. Hotels should be able to provide you with timetables for the citywide system; if not, call the number above.

DRIVING

Almost every hotel on Las Vegas Boulevard South has its own self-parking garage. The best way into these garages, avoiding the gridlock on The Strip, is via the back entrances. Valet parking is also available at the front (and sometimes other) entrances. The standard tip for valets is $2 if they are particularly speedy.

The best advice about driving in Las Vegas is don't do it unless you really have to. The speed limit on The Strip is 35mph (56kph). The wearing of seat belts is compulsory.

MONORAILS
The eagerly awaited state-of-the-art monorail (tel 702/699-8299; www.lvmonorail.com) opened in 2004. Running from MGM Grand to the Sahara, it operates every day from 7am to 2am (Fri–Sun until 3am). It will take you from one end of The Strip to the other in just 15 minutes. There are seven stations: MGM Grand, Bally's/Paris, Flamingo/Caesars, Harrah's/Imperial Palace, Las Vegas Convention Center, Las Vegas Hilton and Sahara. A single fare costs $5, an unlimited one-day pass is $12 and an unlimited three-day pass costs $28. There are also a number of smaller free monorail services courtesy of the hotels, including one between the Mandalay Bay, the Excalibur and the Luxor (every 3–7 minutes, 24 hours), and one between the Mirage and Treasure Island (every 5–15 minutes, 9am–midnight).

TAXIS AND LIMOUSINES
Taxis line up outside every hotel and can be called from your room. When out, you need to call or go to a cab stand; taxis can't be hailed in the street. Taxi drivers have first-hand experience of all the shows and attractions, and can often offer a review and make recommendations. For this service you should give more of a tip than the standard $1 or $2 for a straightforward journey. Also give a bigger tip if they help with the door and your luggage. There are plenty of limousine services, which start at $38 ($55 for a stretch limo) per hour. Your hotel concierge can make the necessary arrangements.
Suggested taxi companies:
ACE Cab Co. 702/736-8383; Checker Cab 702/873-2000; Western Cab Co. 702/736-8000. Limousine Company: Ambassador Limousine 702/362-6200 (toll free 1-888-519-5466).

ORGANIZED SIGHTSEEING
There is no shortage of Vegas-based tour companies offering trips from Vegas to wherever you want to go, but there are also plenty showing the best of the city sights. These tours can give you an insider's view on city attractions, along with a good overview and orientation, before you start exploring independently. Nearly every hotel in Las Vegas has a sightseeing desk from where you can book tours. If the tour bus approach doesn't appeal to you, there are all kinds of other options, including small-scale specialized tours with your own group of family or friends, or using a limousine to whisk you from place to place. Perhaps best of all, you can take to the skies in a helicopter for a bird's-eye view of the fantastic architecture and, on after-dark flights, the glittering lights. Also after dark, a nightclub tour, organized by the Nitelife Tour Company (www.nitetourslasvegas.com) will transport you to the current most popular dance and Latin clubs. The Nitelife Tour Company also offers personalized tours to suit all tastes. Other reputable tour companies include Scenic Airlines (www.scenic.com), Pink Jeep Tours (www.pinkjeep.com) and Look Tours (www.looktours.com).

Essential Facts

MEDICAL TREATMENT

In medical emergencies call ☎ 911 or go to the casualty department of the nearest hospital. Emergency-room services are available 24 hours at University Medical Center (✉ 1800 West Charleston Boulevard ☎ 702/383-2000), or Sunrise Hospital and Medical Center (✉ 3186 Maryland Parkway ☎ 702/731-8000). Pharmacies are indicated by a large green or red cross. Pharmacy telephone numbers are listed under "Pharmacies" or "Drugstores" in the Yellow Pages. Many will deliver medication to your hotel.

24-hour and night pharmacies are available at Walgreens (✉ 1111 Las Vegas Boulevard ☎ 702/471-6840), and at Sav-On (✉ 2300 East Tropicana Avenue ☎ 702/736-4174).

ELECTRICITY

Voltage is 110/120 volts AC (60 cycles) and sockets take two-prong, flat-pin plugs. European appliances also need a voltage transformer.

EMERGENCIES

Police 911
Fire 911
Ambulance 911
American Automobile Association (AAA) breakdown service 800/222-4357.

ETIQUETTE

● Tip staff at least 15–20 percent in a restaurant, taxi drivers $1–$2 for a direct route, porters $1–$2 per bag, depending on the distance carried, and valet parking attendants $2 for speedy service.

● Las Vegas is one of the few pro-smoking places left in the US. Most restaurants have designated smoking areas.

● Dress is very informal during the day, and shorts and T-shirts are generally accepted anywhere. In the evening, smart-casual is more the norm, and some lounges, nightclubs and restaurants may have a dress code.

GAMING

Nevada law permits a wide variety of gaming, but the most popular flutters are roulette, blackjack, craps and slot machines. If you are new to the game, spend some time watching before actually taking the plunge; you could pick up a few tips from the hard-and-fast gamblers. Punters have to be 21 to play. Most casinos do not have windows or clocks, so you are unaware of time passing, and they will often keep you refueled with free drinks and snacks. One benefit of all this cash changing hands is that most of the gaming taxes collected by the state are funneled into public education.

Glossary of terms:

Action Gaming activity measured by the amount wagered.

Bank The person covering the bets in any game, usually the casino.
Buy in Purchasing of chips.
Cage The cashier's section of the casino.
Even money A bet that pays off at one to one.
House edge The mathematical advantage the casino enjoys on every game and wager.
House odds The ratio at which the casino pays off a winning bet.
Limit The minimum/maximum bet accepted at a gambling table.
Loose machine A slot machine set to return a high percentage on the money you put in.
Marker An IOU owed to the casino by someone playing on credit.
Toke A tip or gratuity.

LOST PROPERTY
● For property lost on public transportation: 6675 South Strip Transfer Terminal, South Gillespie Street, tel 702/228-7433; Mon–Fri 8–4.30.
● For property lost at McCarran International Airport: tel 702/261-5134; daily 6.30am–1am.
● Report losses of passports or credit cards to the police.

NATIONAL HOLIDAYS
Jan 1: New Year's Day
3rd Mon in Jan: Martin Luther King Jr. Day
3rd Mon in Feb: President's Day
Mar/Apr: Easter (half-day holiday on Good Friday)
Last Mon in May: Memorial Day
Jul 4: Independence Day
1st Mon in Sep: Labor Day
2nd Mon in Oct: Columbus Day
Nov 11: Veterans' Day
4th Thu in Nov: Thanksgiving
Dec 25: Christmas Day

OPENING HOURS
● Casinos: 24 hours a day, 7 days a week.
● Banks: generally Mon–Fri 9–3 or later, and some Sat mornings.

MONEY

● Credit cards are widely accepted.
● Most banks have ATMs.
● US-dollar traveler's checks are accepted as cash in most places, but ID may be requested.
● Most major hotels will exchange foreign currency, and there are several exchange bureaus on The Strip. You can also change money at major banks.

CURRENCY

The unit of currency is the dollar ($), divided into 100 cents. Bills (notes) are in denominations of $1, $5, $10, $20, $50 and $100. Coins are 1 cent (penny), 5 cents (nickel), 10 cents (dime), 25 cents (quarter) and 50 cents (half dollar).

- Las Vegas has two daily newspapers: the *Las Vegas Review Journal* and the *Las Vegas Sun*.
- Weeklies with club listings and restaurant and bar reviews include *City Life, Las Vegas Magazine, 24/7* and *Las Vegas Weekly*.

TELEPHONES

There are public payphones in hotels, casinos, stores, restaurants, gas stations and on many street corners. You will need a good supply of quarters (overseas calls cost at least $5.50). Local calls from a phone booth cost around 50 cents. Some phones are equipped to take prepaid phone cards and/or charge cards and credit cards. Dial 1 plus the area code for numbers within the United States and Canada. Calls made from hotel rooms are very expensive. Las Vegas's area code is 702, which does not need to be dialed if you are calling within the city. To call Las Vegas from the UK, dial 00 followed by 1 (the code for the US and Canada), then the number. To call the UK from Las Vegas, dial 00 44, then drop the first zero from the area code.

- Post offices: normally Mon–Fri 8.30–6, with limited hours on Sat.
- Stores: usually open at 10am; closing times vary, and may be later on weekends.
- Museums: see individual entries for details.
- Las Vegas boasts that it never closes and never sleeps, but off-Strip stores and banks, and peripheral businesses, will be closed on certain holidays.

POST OFFICES

- Main post office: 1001 East Sunset Road, between Paradise Road and Maryland Parkway, tel 702/361-9349; Mon–Fri 8–9, Sat 8–4. There are many post offices in the city. You can also mail letters and parcels from your hotel.
- Buy stamps from shops and from machines.
- US mailboxes are red and white.

SENSIBLE PRECAUTIONS

Carry only as much money with you as you need; leave other cash and valuables in the hotel safe. At night, avoid hotel parking lots and always enter the hotel via the main entrance. If renting an apartment, use valet parking. Report theft or mugging on the street to the police department immediately. Make sure your room is locked when you leave. Locks can be changed regularly in hotels for security reasons.

STUDENT TRAVELERS

Discounts are sometimes available to students who have an International Student Identity Card (ISIC).

TOILETS

There is never a shortage of clean, free public restrooms to be found throughout the city in hotels, casinos, restaurants and bars.

TOURIST INFORMATION OFFICE

Las Vegas Visitor Information Center: 3150 Paradise Road, Las Vegas, NV 89109, tel 702/892-7575; www.visitlasvegas.com; Mon–Fri 8–5.

Books and Films

BOOKS

Fear and Loathing in Las Vegas by Hunter S. Thompson (1972). Hallucinogenic, drug- and alcoholic-fueled misadventures of "gonzo" journalist Thompson and his deranged lawyer, covering a motorcycle race in Las Vegas. Made into a film (1998), starring Johnny Depp.

Inside Las Vegas by Mario Puzo (1977). Illustrated retrospective of vintage Vegas by *The Godfather* author, with grainy photos revealing the seamier side of life on The Strip.

Literary Las Vegas: The Best Writing about America's Most Fabulous City edited by Mike Tronnes (1995). Anthology of essays and short stories about Vegas mobsters, showgirls, millionaires and celebs, as well as weightier themes such as atomic bomb testing.

When the Mob Ran Vegas by Steve Fischer (2007). Subtitled "Stories of Money, Mayhem and Murder," which sums it up nicely. Gripping anecdotes and inside accounts of the colorful but scary characters who controlled Sin City in the 1950s and 1960s.

FILMS

Ocean's Eleven (1960). Buddies behaving badly, starring Frank Sinatra, Dean Martin and Sammy Davis, Jr., as 11 old friends planning to rob five Vegas casinos in one night

Viva Las Vegas (1964). Grand Prix race driver Lucky Jackson (Elvis Presley) goes off the track to woo pool manageress (Ann Margret), with plenty of singing and dancing.

Rain Man (1988). Conniving Charlie Babbit (Tom Cruise) tries to dupe his autistic savant brother Raymond (Dustin Hoffman) into hitting the jackpot at Caesars Palace.

Indecent Proposal (1993). When David Murphy (Woody Harrelson) loses all his money at a casino table, billionaire John Gage (Robert Redford) offers to pay $1,000,000 for one night with his wife, Diana (Demi Moore).

Casino (1995). Corrupt casino boss Sam Rothstein (Robert De Niro) looks on as his city transforms from mobster empire to family-friendly resort. A powerful Martin Scorsese epic, soaked in blood, power and greed.

SIN CITY

With its origins firmly rooted in vice, corruption and scandal, Las Vegas has always provided a rich source of material for novelists and screenwriters. The weird, the shocking and the extreme are everyday occurrences in real life, re-created in gangster thrillers, such as *Casino*; glitz musicals, like *Viva Las Vegas*; and the escapist road-trip fantasy novel and film *Fear and Loathing in Las Vegas*. And as the ultimate dream of many visitors is to be the lucky one to defy the casino's odds and break the bank— Sin City is likely to be a source of inspiration for many years to come.

NEED TO KNOW

Index

The Automobile Association would like to thank the following photographers, companies and picture libraries for their assistance in the preparation of this book.

Abbreviations for the pictures credits are as follows – (t) top; (b) bottom; (c) center; (l) left; (r) right; (AA) AA World Travel Library.

2t AA/C Sawyer; **2ct** Barbara Kraft/Wynn Las Vegas; **2c** AA/C Sawyer; **2cb** MGM Resorts International; **2b–3t** AA/C Sawyer; **3ct** AA/L Dunmire; **3cb** © Kumar Sriskandan/Alamy; **4t** AA/C Sawyer; **5** © Tibor Bognar/Alamy; **6/7** AA/C Sawyer; **8/9t** AA/L Dunmire; **8/9ctl** AA/C Sawyer; **8/9ctr** Photo Courtesy Caesars Palace Las Vegas; **8/9cbl–8/9b** AA/C Sawyer; **10bl** Getty Images; **10br** Bloomberg via Getty Images; **11** Getty Images; **12** Barbara Kraft/Wynn Las Vegas; **14tl** The Auto Collections, Las Vegas; **14cl–15ct** AA/C Sawyer; **15cb–15tr** The Auto Collections, Las Vegas; **15cr–16l** AA/C Sawyer; **16ct** AA/L Dunmire; **16cb** Mathew Allen; **17tr** AA/L Dunmire; **17cr–18tl** AA/C Sawyer; **18cl** Photo Courtesy Caesars Palace Las Vegas; **19ct–19cb** AA/C Sawyer; **19r** Photo Courtesy Caesars Palace Las Vegas; **20l** AA/L Dunmire; **20/1t–21tr** AA/C Sawyer; **21c–22l** MGM Resorts International; **22r** © Jerry Ballard/Alamy; **22/3c** © Alun Reece/Alamy; **23l** © eye35.co.uk/Alamy; **23r** © Shirley Kilpatrick/Alamy; **24l** MGM Resorts International; **24/5t–24cr** © Kumar Sriskandan/Alamy; **25cl–25tr** MGM Resorts International; **25cr** © David Kilpatrick/ Alamy; **26–27tl** AA/C Sawyer; **27cl** © Sundlof – EDCO/Alamy; **27tr** AA/C Sawyer; **27cr** © PCL/Alamy; **28t–28cl** MGM Resorts International; **28cr–30/1t** AA/C Sawyer; **31cl** © Robert Harding World Imagery/Alamy; **31cr–32–33** AA/C Sawyer; **34l–34cr** Las Vegas Natural History Museum; **35cl** © Bob Pardue – Southwest/Alamy; **35r** Las Vegas Natural History Museum; **36–37** AA/C Sawyer; **38l** MGM Resorts International; **39tl** AA/L Dunmire; **39cl–39cr** MGM Resorts International; **40–41** AA/C Sawyer; **42–43tl** MGM Resorts International; **43ct** AA/C Sawyer; **43cb** © vegas/Alamy; **44–45** The Mob Museum; **46–49** AA/C Sawyer; **50tl** © Lana Sundman/Alamy; **50cl–51cr** AA/C Sawyer; **52l** AA/L Dunmire; **52/3t–55tl** AA/C Sawyer; **55ct–55cr** MGM Resorts International; **56l–56/7t** AA/C Sawyer; **56c** Stratosphere Hotel; **57tr** AA/C Sawyer; **57c** Stratosphere Hotel; **58–61tr** AA/C Sawyer; **61c** AA/L Dunmire; **62l–62/3t** AA/C Sawyer; **62cr** © John Warburton-Lee Photography/ Alamy; **63cl** AA/C Sawyer; **63cr** Wynn Las Vegas; **64** AA/C Sawyer; **66** Courtesy of the Atomic Testing Museum, Las Vegas, Nevada, www.atomictestingmuseum.org; **67bl–69bl** AA/C Sawyer; **69br** Lied Discovery Children's Museum; **70bl** UNLV Marjorie Barrick Museum, 4505 Maryland Parkway, Las Vegas, Nevada, 89154-4012; **70br** © PCL/Alamy; **71bl** AA/Dunmire; **71br** © Steve Bavister/Alamy; **72** © John Elk III/ Alamy; **73bl** Tony n' Tina's Wedding Las Vegas Production; **73br–74bl** AA/C Sawyer; **74br** MGM Resorts International; **75bl** © Niebrugge Images/Alamy; **75br** Springs Preserve; **76bl** © Tibor Bognar/Alamy; **76br** Photodisc; **77–79** AA/C Sawyer; **80** MGM Resorts International; **82** AA/C Sawyer; **83** MGM Resorts International; **86t–86ct** AA/C Sawyer; **86c** AA/L Dunmire; **86cb–88c** AA/C Sawyer; **88b** MGM Resorts International; **89t** AA/C Sawyer; **89b** © Lana Sundman/Alamy; **92–94** AA/C Sawyer; **95t** Barbara Kraft, Wynn Las Vegas; **95b–98t** AA/C Sawyer; **98ct** Stratosphere Hotel; **98cb–98b** AA/C Sawyer; **100c** © PCL/Alamy; **100b** The Mob Museum; **101–104ct** AA/C Sawyer; **104cb** Las Vegas Natural History Museum; **104b** The Mob Museum; **105** AA/C Sawyer; **106c** AA/M Van Vark; **106b–107t** AA/C Sawyer; **107b** 2011 Getty Images; **110–115** AA/C Sawyer; **118** © Richard Green/Alamy; **120–126t** AA/C Sawyer; **126ct** The Wynn, Tomasz and Rosa; **126cb–130** AA/C Sawyer; **133** Penn & Teller; **135** © Aurora Photos/ Alamy; **136** AA/C Sawyer; **138t** ImageState; **138ct–145** AA/C Sawyer; **148** © Kumar Sriskandan/Alamy; **150** AA/C Sawyer; **152t–152c** AA/C Sawyer; **152b** AA/L Dunmire; **154–158** AA/C Sawyer; **160** © Kumar Sriskandan/Alamy.

Every effort has been made to trace the copyright holders, and we apologize in advance for any unintentional omissions or errors. We would be happy to apply any corrections in a following edition of this publication.

Las Vegas' 25 Best

WRITTEN BY Jackie Staddon and Hilary Weston
ADDITIONAL WRITING BY Huw Hennessy
SERIES EDITOR Marie-Claire Jefferies
REVIEWING EDITOR Linda Schmidt
PROJECT EDITOR Karen Kemp
COVER DESIGN Guido Caroti
DESIGN WORK Catherine Murray
INDEXER Joanne Phillips
PICTURE RESEARCHER Liz Allen
IMAGE RETOUCHING AND REPRO Jacqueline Street

ISBN 978-0-307-92808-5

FOURTH EDITION

IMPORTANT TIP
Time inevitably brings changes, so always confirm prices, travel facts, and other perishable information when it matters. Although Fodor's cannot accept responsibility for errors, you can use this guide in the confidence that we have taken every care to ensure its accuracy.

SPECIAL SALES
This book is available for special discounts for bulk purchases for sales promotions or premiums. Special editions, including personalized covers, excerpts of existing books, and corporate imprints, can be created in large quantities for special needs. For more information, write to Special Markets/Premium Sales, 1745 Broadway, 3-2, New York, NY 10019 or email specialmarkets@randomhouse.com.

Color separation by AA Digital Department
Printed and bound by Leo Paper Products, China

10 9 8 7 6 5 4 3 2 1

Cover image: Konstantin Sutyagin/Shutterstock

A04634
Maps in this title produced from map data supplied by Global Mapping, Brackley, UK © Global Mapping
Transport map © Communicarta Ltd, UK

Titles in the Series